About the Author

Gareth Lewis, a veteran psychic medium with over 26 years of experience, facilitates connections with departed loved ones. He has worked extensively across venues in the UK and Europe. Gareth's expertise enables healing, understanding, and progression on spiritual paths. Believing in the profound impact of connections, he delivers insightful readings, empowering clients and audiences alike. His transformative journey began when he sought solace in a spiritualist church, an experience that redirected his life's purpose. Embracing development classes and delivering mediumship demonstrations, Gareth passionately shares his life-transforming gift, believing that the spiritualist church saved him. He strives to continue impacting others' lives positively.

Spirit, Can You Hear Me?

Best Wishes

Gareth Lewis

Spirit, Can You Hear Me?

Olympia Publishers
London

www.olympiapublishers.com
OLYMPIA PAPERBACK EDITION

A CIP catalogue record for this title is
available from the British Library.

ISBN: 978-1-83543-198-6

This book is a memoir. It reflects the author's present recollections of
experiences over time. Some names and characteristics have been
changed, some events have been compressed, and some dialogue
has been recreated.

First Published in 2025

Olympia Publishers
Tallis House
2 Tallis Street
London
EC4Y 0AB

Printed in Great Britain

Dedication

I would like to dedicate this book to my partner, Kelly and my two sons, Jack and James. Kelly has been a great source of support and love throughout all the ups and downs in my life and my journey as a psychic medium. She has been there to encourage, motivate, and listen to me when I needed it most, even when I felt like giving up. Jack and James have been my source of strength and love; they are my greatest achievement, and I am so proud of the strong, independent men they have become. Without their love and support, I would not have been able to carry on. My love for them has been my greatest motivation to get up each day. Kelly and the boys have been there for me every step of the way, through my good and dark times, and for that, I am truly grateful.

Acknowledgements

I am immensely grateful to all those who contributed to the creation of this book, directly or indirectly. Their support, guidance, and encouragement have been invaluable throughout this journey.

I am deeply indebted to several remarkable individuals whose support, wisdom, and guidance have been pivotal in the creation of this book. Among them, Katherine Hill, your unwavering belief in this project from its inception to completion has been an incredible source of motivation. For the many hours you have spent writing this book, I will be forever grateful.

To Violet Bradley MBE, your invaluable assistance and expertise have been instrumental in shaping the essence and depth of this book. Your remarkable insights and contributions have elevated the content and added a profound richness to its narrative. Your generosity in sharing your wisdom has made an indelible mark on these pages.

To my partner, Kelly, thank you for your help in putting this book together and your patience with me, especially when trying to get the information you needed out of me. I know at times your patience was stretched. I extend my heartfelt gratitude to all three of you for your selfless dedication, invaluable support, and tireless efforts in assisting me throughout the writing process. Your contributions have been immeasurable and have significantly enriched the quality of this work.

Finally, I would also like to express my appreciation and

gratitude to Michelle Sciama for allowing me to tell her and Daniella's story.

This book is a product of collective efforts and the remarkable contributions of Katherine Hill, Kelly McGuire, Violet Bradley MBE, and many others. I am profoundly grateful for your guidance, patience, and belief in this endeavour.

PREFACE

I first began writing this book as a way of expressing my thoughts and feelings. With so much anger written amongst the bad language in an old notebook, the story of my life unfolded, and I began to understand why I am the way I am. It has taken this long as I never thought about it being published until I read it again some years later. Using this notebook as guidance, I wrote of all my experiences—some good and some very hard to talk about—as well as addressing my mental health, and how it has affected me for many years, and how I try to keep it separate from my work as a medium.

It was while writing this book I realised something important. As someone who is very sensitive and has always taken things to heart, and has been bullied for most of their life, I have now—especially in this age of social media, where people can hide behind a screen to say what they want regardless of how it may affect others—put themselves into the public arena, doing a job many people don't agree with. If unhappy with what you do and how you work, people will tell you and share their opinions of you with the world.

Many of us wear a mask to hide a multitude of emotions and sins. I wear mine so nobody knows the real me—how shy and lacking in confidence I truly am. I know what you may think: How can someone who is shy and self-critical stand in front of an audience of hundreds of people without a script, not knowing what's going to happen, and second-guessing what they think of him? The answer is, "I trust in the power of the spirit, even though I may not trust in myself." I hide behind the mask I have created to protect myself. Now, it's time to come from behind the mask, and by doing so, if I only help just one person by writing this book, it will have been worth all the tears and memories I have shared with you.

CHAPTER 1

The Daughter

"No matter the distance between this world and the next, my love for you shines eternally." - Gareth Lewis

It was a serene Saturday afternoon, the gentle sunlight filtering through the lace curtains of my sitting room, casting a soft glow upon the cosy space. Seated across from me were my clients, two women whose presence held a delicate balance of sorrow and anticipation. The two ladies who were here to communicate with me, the Medium. The first lady was more mature, elegantly dressed, yet there was an air of palpable sadness about her. The second lady was younger, much more excited, and eager to speak.

Did I say they were here to communicate with me, the Medium? What I should have said is that they were here to communicate with each other, as this was a mother whose daughter was now in the world of spirit. Did I just say that there were two women waiting to speak to each other in my sitting room and one of them had 'died'? Can people in the world of spirit really come back and tell us they are okay?

I'm getting ahead of myself, so let me explain.

The lady in my sitting room was Michelle, who had arrived hoping to communicate with her daughter. As I could see her standing next to Michelle, it was only a matter of time before she spoke to me. When a person in the world of spirit is ready to communicate through me, energy builds up in the room, and I feel a strong sense of power and what I can only describe as a wave of love surrounding me. Today was no exception, and Michelle's daughter was about to speak.

I said, "As I see your daughter, she's beautiful, with long brunette hair, and about five feet five inches tall, and in her late teens, with a beautiful smile." Michelle's face lit up as I accurately described her daughter, who was now telling me she had been unable to breathe. Recounting this to Michelle, she nodded in acknowledgement, as grief had stolen her words, and she was unable to speak. I continued, giving more and more evidence of what I saw, heard, and sensed, describing how she collapsed and passed to the world of spirit. Michelle sobbed and confirmed that she understood all the information I had recounted.

I gave Michelle a moment to breathe and turned to her daughter, asking, "What else you would like your mum to know?" "Tell her she has left my room the same and supported me with my studies. Please tell her I'm okay and that I didn't die." As I recounted this to Michelle, a faint smile crossed her tear-soaked face. This was her daughter; she had survived death, and this was enough information for Michelle to know her daughter was still with her.

As the reading ended, Michelle sank into her chair and began to tell me about her daughter, who had passed at the tender age of eighteen from a major asthma attack, which had happened in a nail bar where she had gone to get her nails done. Although time had passed since it happened, she was still struggling to come to terms with it.

I remember thinking that I would never be able to come to terms with such a devastating event, and my heart was wrenched apart as I looked at this lady, who was utterly broken and desperately trying to hold herself together.

Later that day, I could not get Michelle and her daughter out of my mind, and so I spoke to my partner about them (not something that I would normally do, as all private readings are just that, private!) It's just that this lady and her daughter had a profound impact on me, and I felt the need to get it off my chest. Losing a child is the most unimaginable grief, and I knew it would not be the last time I would see her.

A couple of months later, Michelle visited me for another reading, followed by a second and then a third over the next few months. I became concerned that she was relying too much on Mediums, and so when she tried to book a fourth, I realised that I would have to intervene and tell her it would be better if she left a little more time between her readings, as I couldn't guarantee that her daughter would come through every time. I told her she needed to make some time for herself and not to be so focused on private readings, as her daughter would only come through when she had something to say.

I had to be honest and tell her that the more I learned about her daughter from every meeting we had, the greater the possibility that I might mix up that knowledge with any new evidence I was receiving.

Michelle took on board everything I told her, and now I see her a couple of times a year. Each time she comes, I see a little bit of an improvement in how she is coping. She is such a brave lady, and I am proud to know her. Michelle is never far from my thoughts, and I look forward to her visits. She is an example of how great courage and determination can overcome even the deepest despair.

To give real insight into my life, I think I need to start at the beginning. How did all this begin?

CHAPTER 2

Beginnings

"And the soul blossomed, growing ever stronger in wisdom and grace." - Gareth Lewis

I was born Gareth Thomas Pimbley on 10th June 1971 at Haslam's Maternity Home in Bolton, Lancashire. It was a Thursday, and my mum, Joyce, was at home in Horwich, which is a village just outside of Bolton in the northwest of England. As she loaded the washing machine, the contractions began, so she calmly phoned for an ambulance and travelled to the maternity unit alone. My dad, Tom, opted to stay home and take care of my two-year-old brother, Lee. It was the day before my mum's 21st birthday, but no matter how much she'd hoped for it, I was in no mood to wait for her big day to make my appearance, so I made my entrance into the world at 7:25 p.m., weighing a hefty 9 lb 5 oz.

Meanwhile, Dad had found himself a babysitter and made it down to the hospital for visiting, but much to his chagrin, he was promptly capped and gowned and shoved into the delivery room—despite his protests—by the midwife, just in time to witness the arrival of his second son. Mum later told me he was more interested in the contents of the bucket containing my afterbirth than he was in the big event, but at least he was there, no matter how reluctantly.

When I was young, my mum was the centre of my universe.

She was always there to look after me and my brother, and I loved her so very much. Dad worked at the local Loco works, so he was always at work or in the pub. As we were growing up, he always seemed a little distant.

There were, of course, other family members who were constantly in and out of our lives. Mum had two sisters and a brother. Auntie Val was the oldest, and she lived in a place called Southport, a small seaside town in the northwest of England. We only saw her now and again, but I always got the impression that she was ashamed of where she came from. I may have been wrong, but that's what I thought. Auntie Val had two children, a son and a daughter, but as they were a lot older than me, I don't remember them much.

Auntie Marg, the second oldest, was completely different. She was very open and friendly, just like an auntie should be. She lived in Newquay, Cornwall, so we used to spend Christmas together—one year in Horwich, and the next in Newquay. As we got older, we would travel down to Newquay to spend the summer with Marg and her family. There were three children in Marg's family: two boys and a girl. I always thought they were spoiled, so we didn't really get on that well, especially the youngest, Tristan. He was a few years younger than me and a bit of a brat—well, to me, anyway. He would get up to all kinds of mischief and then blame me, and I would get into trouble for something I hadn't done.

The youngest of Mum's siblings was Uncle John. He was in the RAF and stationed at Anglesey in Wales; he was an Air Traffic Controller and a bit of a joker. He liked nothing better than playing pranks on people. Uncle John married a Welsh girl called Annetta, and we all travelled to Wales for the wedding. My grandma was really excited because she thought that all

Welsh people were superb singers, and I think she expected something akin to the Welsh voice choir singing at the church! However, she was in for a big disappointment, as all she got was a few parishioners and Annetta's family singing the hymns, and to be honest, they were pretty awful. John and Annetta had two sons and eventually got based in Germany, so we didn't see them much after that.

It was at a young age that I discovered Uncle John could leave his body. Astral travel, for those who don't already know, is an out-of-body experience through which the consciousness can function separately from the physical body. So, in a nutshell, the soul can leave the body. I always knew Uncle John was special in a spiritual way, and it was common knowledge within the family that he had this gift. On one occasion, when he had just started his career in the RAF and was feeling extremely homesick, after a hard day at work, he decided that later that evening, when everyone had gone back to the dorm for lights out, settled, and gone to sleep, he was going to astral travel home to see his mum and dad at their home in Bolton. He began by going into a deep meditation to enable his soul to leave his physical body. Within just a few moments, he was standing in the living room back home, taking in everything he could see and feeling a sense of normality as his parents were sat watching TV as they always did after a busy day. The next day, he phoned his mum and explained what had happened the night before, recounting everything he could see, even down to what they were wearing and the conversation they were having about going to the garden centre at the weekend. Although my grandma was very proud of her only son's spiritual gift and appreciated that he was homesick, she told Uncle John it wasn't appropriate to eavesdrop and turn up in such an unannounced way. Uncle John had many such experiences before he sadly died at the young age of thirty-eight of a brain tumour.

My maternal grandparents, Grandma and Grandad Lewis, lived in a council house overlooking a field with horses in Bolton. Grandma was a very spiritual lady and, on occasions, read people's palms. She worked as a cook in a school kitchen, and she also worked as a housekeeper. She was very elegant, with olive skin and dark, wavy hair, and she had a very caring nature. I will always remember what a fantastic cook she was and the delicious pies and cakes that she made. She taught me how to bake when I was young, and for a long time after that, I had the ambition to become a chef. Grandad was a quiet man; he was very clever and worked as an engineer, and I have fond memories of helping him in the garden, but as he wasn't much of a conversationalist, I wasn't as close to him as I was to Grandma. I have frequently been told of the striking resemblance I have to Grandad Lewis.

Grandma and Grandad Pimbley, Dad's parents, lived locally, so we saw them all the time, and they were a big part of our lives. Grandma had strawberry blonde hair, which was always arranged in a chic bouffant 1950s style. She was tall and slim and always wore a blue nylon housecoat. She always had fig rolls for us, and they were my very favourite biscuit, but I got the impression that my mum didn't like her much. Grandad was a small, olive-skinned man, his black hair sleeked back with Brylcreem and covered with a flat cap, which he even wore in the house. He loved to sit in his chair and watch Grandma run around after his every whim. When she wasn't looking, he would entertain me and Lee by pushing his dentures in and out of his mouth. Occasionally, Grandma would see him, and she would tell him off.

Our home was a large terraced house with a bay window and three bedrooms. It was a quiet residential street in the heart of the town, or village, as some people liked to call it. When I was a month old, we were all set to go on a family holiday to Devon to stay in a caravan by the sea. I say all set because I never actually got to go on that holiday. The day before we were to set off on our adventure, my mum had put me outside in my pram, as people did in those days, while she got my brother Lee dressed when a small girl from across the road climbed up onto the pram and pulled me out onto the ground. Hearing my screams, my mum was frantic. She came rushing out of the house to find me lying face down on the cold concrete path. I was immediately rushed off to the doctor, who proclaimed that I was perfectly fine, but this did not convince my grandma, who demanded that I be left at home in her care, just in case. The rest of the family set off without me.

CHAPTER 3

The Early Years

"The darkest times hold the power to fuel the brightest future."
- Gareth Lewis

I was baptised into the Christian faith at Horwich Parish Church as both my parents were members of the Church of England. When I was three years old, I went to Fox Street Nursery and then on to Chorley New Road Infants at five. They were happy years, but my memories of those early years have faded. My days at infant school were happy ones too, and I would often sit contented and alone with my back against the wall that ran around the playground. One day, after deciding to abandon my perch and run around the playground with my friends, my nose encountered Sharon Pattison's head at full throttle, and guess who came off worst? Me, of course! I sat in school all afternoon with a blue paper towel held up to my nose, largely ignored by the teachers. As no one informed my parents of the incident, when my mum came to collect me at the end of the school day, she was told that I was involved in a little accident. She pulled the paper towel away from my face and exclaimed, "That's not a bit of an accident, he's got a broken nose!" Grabbing my hand, she marched indignantly out of the playground and straight home, where she sought the advice of Mr Johnson, the resident ambulance driver and medical expert to all. Confirming my mum's suspicions that it was indeed broken, I was taken to the

Accident and Emergency Department at the Bolton Royal Infirmary. To this day, I still have problems with my nose from that little encounter. I was always accident-prone and would often go to my grandma's house to be looked after.

On one occasion, when Grandma was caring for me, I was not feeling well that day and took the day off from school. I lay on the settee with a blanket placed over me and watched cartoons on her old imitation wood surround television in the corner of the room. As I watched the cartoons, I noticed I could hear voices in the kitchen. I have always been a little nosy and scared of missing out on something, so it intrigued me to know what was going on and who she was talking to. I quietly got myself off the settee and made my way to the kitchen. She was sitting at the table with three old ladies. I say old. They were old to me, as I was just a child. I stood peering from behind the door, not wanting to be noticed but curious about what was happening. They had just finished drinking their cup of tea when she took her friend's hand and read her palm, explaining what she could see. "I see your husband up a ladder," she said. "Oh, right, he will be doing some work on the gutters," the lady replied quickly.

Grandma went silent, her eyes staring intensely at her palm, then abruptly let go with a shocked look in her eyes. "That's all I see," she explained. I knew that whatever was going on, it was ending, so I quickly scurried back into the living room and took my position back on the settee. I could hear the ladies being ushered out of the house when Grandma came in to check on me.

A few weeks had passed when, on a warm summer's day, my grandma got a knock on the door. Standing before her was the lady from a few weeks before. Noticing that she was visibly upset, she was invited to come in, and they sat in the kitchen. The lady told her that just a few days ago, her husband had been doing some repairs to their house. She told her that whilst fixing the gutter, the ladders had slipped, and he had fallen to his death. Remembering what had been said a few weeks earlier, Grandma was upset at what, not only had been recounted but she had seen in this lady's palm: the ladders on the ground and a man dead next to them. From that day on, she read no one's palm again.

I remember the day when my parents told me they were getting a divorce. I was seven years old when Mum sat me and my brother down and explained we would no longer live with our dad and would move house. Now, you may think that I would be devastated by this—the divorce, not the move, but I wasn't really. My dad was a bit of a distant figure in my life… and still is. He was either at work or at the pub getting drunk, and I know that my mum put up with a lot from him until she had finally had enough. Sometimes I think she was like a single parent to me and my brother, but with the added hassle of having a petulant adult living with us. So, me, my mum, and Lee moved out of Penn Street and went to stay with Grandma and Grandad Lewis for a couple of weeks while Mum tried to get things sorted. After a short period of staying with my grandparents, Mum found work. The family home was sold, and we moved into a two-bedroom flat at the other end of Horwich. Mum would work all day and then come home to get changed and go out again to her second job at a pub, leaving me with my brother, who was getting resentful at having to look after me all the time. He wanted to be out with his friends, so he would sneak out, leaving me alone. The loneliness and isolation I felt as a child still haunt me. I spent a lot of time alone as I didn't have many friends, and there was never anyone at home. School was also a trial, often sitting by myself, not really interacting with other children. They bullied me… a lot!

One afternoon I was leaving school when 'Briggsy' and his gang of bullies were waiting for me by an old oak tree by the school entrance. My heart sank as I knew they were going to follow me home, call me names, attempt to trip me up, and then beat me. I did not know how to defend myself, telling no one of the abuse they subjected me to through fear that if I spoke out, the beatings would get worse. They knew my secret, the thing that I was trying to hide, which they could see. They knew I was different—'weird', even—and I was ashamed and afraid. Let me explain what I mean. I was not only a very shy person, but I was much taller than the other children of my age and extremely thin and gangly. I was just awkward-looking, which made me an easy target.

My feelings of insecurity followed me home, and often my brother couldn't wait to get out of the house when he should have been taking care of me. From the age of ten, my spiritual awareness was becoming more apparent. I think I freaked him out, and I guess he was a little scared of being alone with me. He didn't understand my gift, which would often manifest with physical phenomena. I would stare at the curtains and ask spirit to move them, and they would, on my command. We also had an ornamental grandfather clock. It was about five inches tall and didn't work because it had no working parts inside. It was an empty shell, but when we were alone, I would set the hands to the correct time, and it would keep going to the correct time all day! One day, the clock disappeared, and although he denied it, I'm sure that Lee threw it out because it scared him.

As a teenager, to earn a little extra money, I had a paper round which involved collecting my bag of newspapers from Mr Althrop, a lovely gentleman who ran the local newsagents. One evening, at the end of my round, the light was fading. I was glad

I had only one house to deliver to before I could go home. The house was large, old, and at the end of a long drive surrounded by trees. I was filled with dread as I knew the bullies had followed me and were hiding in the trees waiting to attack and beat me to a pulp, which they did frequently, and yet still, I stayed silent.

A boy in my class discovered what was going on. I don't know how, because I never told him, but he insisted he come with me on my paper round from then on. So, that evening, he came with me to collect my paper bag from Mr Althrop as usual. It was now our last delivery, the old house. My heart was racing, it filled me with anxiety. What was going to happen? Was this going to make this situation worse? Would they attack us both? My mind was filled with fear.

As we walked through the tree-lined drive from the old house, there they were. They were waiting, and as they jumped out at me; It shocked them to see that I wasn't alone. What happened next is a lesson I remember to this day. A look of horror ran across 'Briggsy's' face as the reality struck that I was ready to fight back. Within a split second, 'Briggsy' ran, and his gang of bullies followed.

Sometimes in life, we can often be faced with lessons which help us to grow, and sometimes we repeat those lessons. I am no exception. Time passed and, now an adult, I was living alone in my flat and finding it a bit of a struggle to make ends meet, so I advertised for a flatmate. Guess who replied to the advert? It was none other than 'Briggsy', the bully who had made my life such a misery in those early years. He had split from his girlfriend and was homeless, and I felt a sense of pity. I stared at him for a moment, and to this day, I do not know why I didn't slam the door in his face. It must have been my spiritual side and my soft heart, but I agreed to take him in, as I couldn't see someone on the streets, and so he rented a room from me. My friends and family all thought I was mad for allowing him into my home, given how much misery he had caused me during my younger years. It was not one of my better decisions. He hadn't changed at all, and it was no surprise that his relationship was troubled, resulting in his girlfriend throwing him out. He was still the immature little bully, only not so little now.

I tolerated him for a couple of years, during which he would do anything to avoid of paying rent. He treated my flat as if it was his own and tried to manipulate me once again. One day, I came home to find the front door and all the windows were open, but there was no sign of him. This was the catalyst that finally opened my eyes to his behaviour, and my blood boiled. How could I have been so naïve as to allow this vile person back into my life? Everyone had tried to warn me, but I just didn't listen. Well, I was listening now, and enough was enough. He eventually returned home, and I told him in no uncertain terms to get his stuff and get out. When he squared up to me and sneered, ready to start his usual bullying tactics. But something in my face must have stopped him because he shrank back into himself. He was no longer facing that frightened little boy of all those years ago but a fully grown man who was bigger than he was and who had finally found his courage. I would like to think that it was me alone who made him leave that day, but I must concede that the timely arrival of my friend probably had something to do with it too. That was the last I saw of 'Briggsy'.

As I grew up, my psychic experiences dwindled until they practically disappeared altogether, probably because I was suppressing them as my life became more difficult as a young adult. Not everything was doom and gloom, however, and I have happy memories of my childhood, too.

My mum fancied herself as a bit of a psychic, and on a Friday evening, she would set the table out for her weekly séance. They placed handwritten letters and numbers arranged around the edge of the table, with an upturned glass in the centre. As friends arrived, they took their seats at the table, placing one finger on the glass and calling out, 'Is there anyone there?' One Friday, I hid behind the couch to watch what was going on. It all started as usual: the light went off, fingers on the glass, hearing the obligatory 'Is there anyone there?' As I looked into the corner of the room, the shadows seemed to thicken, and I sat in fear as a mist began to build and take shape. Slowly, the figure of a man emerged, his face filled with rage. Could everyone see what I saw, or was it just me?

A terrifying scream broke the silence as the glass shot off the table and shattered against the wall. The man had vanished, and the gathering dispersed into the front room, still shaken from the experience. Who was this man full of rage? I never found out, as I slinked back to bed, vowing never to take part in one of my mum's Friday séances again.

The next Friday, the crowd gathered in the kitchen once more for their weekly fright, but this time there was a new face— a medium who had been invited to show the group how to conduct a séance correctly. Her name was Mrs Holden, and little did I know then, but in later years this lady would have a massive impact on my spiritual life and help me in so many ways to develop as a medium.

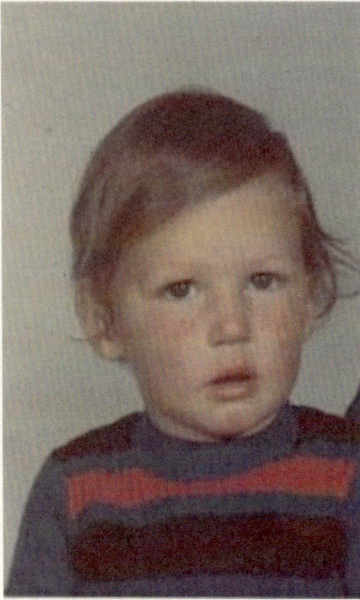

The Early Years

CHAPTER 4

Dolls

"Sometimes the shadows whisper what the light dares not reveal." - Gareth Lewis

Living with my grandparents for that short period was quite difficult for Mum, having to pack up all her belongings with two children in tow and moving back in with her parents. Even though we were welcomed to stay there, you got the real feeling it was only for a short time. My grandparents, although they loved us, made it known that they had brought up their children and didn't relish the thought of Lee and I running around their house.

My grandparents lived in a three-bedroom house on a council estate in Bolton. The house was immaculate, everything clean and tidy and in its place. As soon as you walked through the front door, you were greeted with the smell of cakes or bread baking in the oven. While living there, they gave us the job of cleaning the brass that would hang over the fireplace—a dirty job, I know, but I didn't mind; I quite enjoyed it. Our room was at the top of the stairs, next to the bathroom. I would always run up the stairs as it was quite dark and narrow. Even with the light on, the fashion of the day was dark wallpaper with a brown patterned carpet going up the stairs. The room Lee and I shared was small, with only a single bed and a small set of drawers in it, but it was OK; we didn't need anything else. We would top and tail. I always slept at the bottom end of the bed underneath the two shelves on the wall. This is where Grandma's dolls lived. Growing up, Grandma never had a doll and always wanted one of her own. So, for a birthday present, Grandad bought her one. It was a porcelain doll with light hair, wearing a summery dress. Grandma was over the moon with it, putting it in pride of place on the shelf Grandad had put up specially for the doll. Thinking it looked quite lonely sitting there in the spare room, Grandma bought a couple more to keep it company.

They were three of the ugliest dolls you could imagine. The dolls always made me feel uncomfortable, as if they were staring at you, watching you as you slept. I didn't want to sleep in that room, but with nowhere else to sleep and Grandma refusing to move them, saying it was their room and I was just being silly, I had little choice. Trying not to look at them, I would quickly put on my pyjamas, jump into bed, and place the thick, itchy blanket over my head and go to sleep.

One night I was woken by Lee's voice whispering, "Gareth wake up, wake up." My eyes flicked open, and he hissed, "Look at the dolls." My head turned towards the dolls above my head, and sure enough, there in the moonlight from the chink in the curtains, it was plain to see the three dolls were dancing on the shelf. I darted to the other end of the bed, gripping onto Lee as hard as I could. We pulled the covers up over our heads and, after what seemed like an eternity, peeked out from our hiding place, and they were sat back down in their usual places on the shelf. Frightened by what had just happened, I told Lee I was sleeping next to him from now on. There was no argument from him; I think he wanted the same. This would happen every night. Sometimes we couldn't go straight to sleep as we waited for the dolls to come alive again. It is only now, as an adult, that I realise it was the spirit moving the dolls and not that the dolls were possessed. To this day, those dolls are currently sitting in my Mum's bedroom and still terrify me. Mum says she is leaving them to me in her will!

The Dancing Dolls

CHAPTER 5

Finding Spirit

"Finding spirit is like discovering a quiet hand in the dark, reminding you that you are never truly alone." - Gareth Lewis

When I was eighteen, I started working in a small video rental shop in my hometown of Horwich. After only a few months of working there, they offered me the job of manager I was so excited and accepted the position straight away. It wasn't an overly busy shop, and over time I got to recognise most of the customers as they came in. I learned what films they liked and was on hand to help in any way I could. One perk of the job was that we got to watch the films first.

One day, a young lady walked in—quite petite with short blonde hair—whom I had never seen before. I asked if there was anything I could recommend for her to watch. We instantly clicked, and that day, when she walked into the shop, she also walked into my life. The connection between us was so strong that as soon as I set eyes on her, I knew we would be together. As time went by, she became the focus of my very existence, and we spent every spare moment together.

Mum was very strict about who my brother and I brought into the house and at what times, so we spent most of our courtship sitting in her car, a champagne-coloured D-reg Mini, at the front of the house, talking late into the night. We had been dating for about a year when we set up a home together. By this point, I had left the video shop and started working on the markets for a family-run business selling tights, stockings, and ladies' lingerie, of all things. Even though the days were long and hard, especially in the winter months when the weather was biting cold, I enjoyed what I was doing. There was a social side to the job. When we were not serving customers, we would often stand with other stallholders chatting about different things with a warm drink and having a laugh. The family I was working for not only had market stalls, but also had several shops. One was local and had a flat above it, which had just become vacant, so it was perfect for us, and we soon settled in.

There was, however, a cloud on our horizon in the form of her father. He really didn't approve of our relationship. He was a very well-respected surgeon at the local hospital and had his own private practice. He had worked hard to give his family the best of everything in life, and I was just not good enough for his daughter. There I was, a badly educated nobody who worked on the markets, with no prospects, no direction, and no future as far as he could see. But I was determined to prove him wrong. Okay, maybe I didn't have the best job in the world, but it paid the bills, and I was only young, so it was only a matter of time until I found my true path in life—I was sure of it. A couple of years later, much to her father's disapproval, we got married. It was 1993, and I was twenty-two years old. It was at this point in my life, I decided after so many years of my dad being in and out of my life, I didn't want to get married with his surname, so I changed my last name from Pimbley to my mum's maiden name of Lewis by Deed Poll.

The night before the wedding, I had what I can describe only as a spiritual intervention when I was overcome by intense doubt about what I was about to do, but I put it down to pre-wedding nerves. I had not yet learned to listen to the messages being given to me by the spirit world, so went to bed. When I awoke the next day, the feelings were stronger than ever, and I was consumed by a sense that our relationship was doomed. I brushed my feelings aside and got ready for our wedding. After all, what could go wrong? We loved each other.

Not long after getting married, we moved from the flat into a house we had bought together and settled down to married life. I would often return home from work exhausted, and our romantic life had turned into evenings in front of the fire watching television, where I would often fall asleep and she would be left to her own company. Not a great start, I know, but if I worked hard, things would eventually get better—I was convinced of it.

I had been interested in the spiritual side of life from an early age, so when given a pack of Tarot cards, it seemed like the ideal time to reignite my interest. So, I began to understand more about not only how to use them and what they can be used for. I soon learnt that Tarot can be a powerful tool to use. I never believed someone could foretell the future, but I believed we are writing our own future, and through their choices, others can influence what is going to happen in our life. By using the cards, you can discover how to make positive changes and manifest your goals and your dreams for the future.

After a while and understanding more about how to use them, I started practicing on my friends and family, who were all very keen for me to give them a 'reading'. I was giving a Tarot reading to my wife. We were sitting on the floor in the front room. The fire was flickering in the hearth, giving the room an eerie glow. I handed her the pack of cards, and she shuffled them a few times. As I watched her, I had an odd, uneasy feeling about what I was about to see in her cards. As she handed them back to me, the feeling intensified, my heart pounding. I dealt the top three cards onto the floor in front of her and turned the first one over. The fire crackled, and the shadow of the flames flickered across her face, I looked down at the card—it was a Page. The blood was pounding in my ears as I heard myself say "Watch out for a man called Joe. I have a bad feeling about him."

"We don't know anyone called Joe," she replied.

"I know," I said, "but I have this really strong feeling that something bad is going to happen concerning this person, and you really need to stay away from him." She looked at me as if I had gone mad and got up and left the room. I picked up the card and stared at it for a long time.

Life carried on as normal for the next six months when she got a new job at the same company where my brother worked. It was a department store in Bolton, and this is where she met Joe. It wasn't long before they started having an affair, and after a few months of sneaking around behind my back; she announced that our marriage was over and she was moving in with Joe. My world disintegrated before my eyes, and I turned to my family for support. One night, as we were talking, my brother admitted to me that he had been suspicious that something was going on between them for a while and he had even confronted them about it at work. They both denied it, of course, and he hadn't told me because he didn't have any proof. I realised that Lee had been put in an impossible position, so I didn't blame him for not telling me. After all, I probably have done the same thing in his position. After a few weeks of begging and pleading with her to come back, I finally had to face the truth. There was no way back. My marriage was over, and that was when my life fell apart. I stopped eating and sleeping and spent my days crying and mulling over what I had lost, spiralling into a pit of despair with depression dragging me down to a place I never want to see again. I had always been quite thin, but now my weight crashed down to 10 stones and finally to an all-time low of 7 1/2 stones as my dark thoughts reached one inevitable conclusion: suicide.

One terrible night, after lying in the dark staring at the ceiling, I got up and went downstairs to get a knife, as I had to end the misery once and for all. I walked into the kitchen, opened the drawer, and picked up the largest, sharpest knife l owned. I turned to walk back to the stairs, sat down on the bottom step, and tensed myself to do it. People say that suicide is the coward's way out, but I know this is not true. It is depression that drives you into that state of mind, and sheer despair that drives the sword, so to speak. Luckily for me, it was the fear that this would turn out to be just another one of my endless failures.

I awoke the next morning, my eyes puffy and swollen from crying. It was a Sunday. The street outside was quiet and still. My eyes moved to the clock on the bedside table, but they couldn't quite focus on the time. I tried to move but I couldn't; I was paralysed with a fear greater than I had ever known gripping my heart. I was alone in the house, so there was no one I could call out to for help. My eyes searched frantically around the room in search of the phone, but I couldn't see it and I still couldn't move to find it. "Oh God," I thought, "I'm going to die here alone," and finally I realised I didn't want to die—not here, not like this, alone and still so young. After what seemed like an hour, I moved my arm enough to feel for the phone on the bedside table and tapped out the numbers to reach my mum. She had recently moved to Norfolk with her new partner and was frantic when I told her what had happened, not just for what had happened that morning but also for what I told her had happened the night before. I put the phone down so that Mum could phone for my brother to visit me, as it was too far for her to get there anytime soon. Lee arrived with a look of fear in his eyes, not knowing what he was going to walk into, and quickly called for the doctor. When the doctor arrived, and after talking with me, he soon realised I had suffered a mental breakdown and sent me to the local psychiatric hospital to be assessed.

As Lee drove me to the hospital, the car was in deadly silence. I glanced across at my brother, struggling for something to say to break the tension I could feel building up around us, but his eyes were locked on the road ahead. I shrank back down into my seat and kept quiet. Upon arrival at the hospital, we checked in and were shown to a waiting area. It was in a corridor just off the ward, and we could see the patients wandering around. Some were chatting quietly to themselves, rocking backwards and forwards as they paced the corridor. Others were shouting and gesticulating frantically at some hidden adversary. I could feel the blood pounding in my ears. "Oh God, please don't let me have to stay here," I thought. I looked over at Lee; his face was pale, and the shock at what we were witnessing was plain to see. "Is this what you want?" he hissed. "Is this where you want to be?" I averted my eyes and looked down at the floor, suppressing the tears so that he wouldn't see how scared I was. The nurse eventually arrived and took us in to see the doctor, who, after a quick assessment, confirmed that I was having a breakdown and would need constant care and support to get through it.

Somehow, Lee convinced the doctor that I would be better off with our Mum, that he would take me down to Norfolk to stay with her for a while rather than to be in the hospital, away from my family and everyone who cared for me. By some miraculous reason, the doctor agreed and said that it would be a good idea. I could never thank my brother enough for supporting me, and I realised at that moment just how much my family meant to me and how much I loved them. Once we got outside the hospital, though, Lee turned to me, his face twisted with rage. He pushed me up against the wall and said, "Don't you ever get yourself into such a state that we have to come back here again, do you understand?" I nodded, and he turned to walk away. I knew then that I had to sort my life out and stop hurting the people who loved me. I left for Norfolk the next day.

After a few months of my Mum's care, I returned home, not to my marital home—that would have been too much—but to my Mum's flat, which, luckily, she had kept on after she had moved down to Norfolk. I still cried myself to sleep most nights, but I kept the depression at bay, and slowly, a little of normality returned to my life. I eventually went back to work, and one day, while in the warehouse where the stock was stored, I felt a little emotional, so I went to find a quiet corner where I could sit and be alone for a minute. Suddenly, I had a strong feeling that my grandmother, who had passed eight years earlier, was there with me. I missed her so much when she died, but I had never felt her presence before, and the thought that she was still with me filled my heart with hope. Unfortunately, that hope didn't last very long and within days, I had that overwhelming desire to end it all. I felt completely and utterly hopeless. I realised that the depression, what I now call the monster, was back.

Feeling alone and what I can only explain as 'ashamed' for feeling like this, and not wanting to go back to the psychiatric ward for fear they would keep me in this time, I didn't tell anyone. That evening, I left my flat with the sole intention of ending my life, with no plan on how I was going to do it or even where. I just knew I couldn't carry on feeling this way. An hour went by, just walking around debating how I should take my life. I noticed the lights were on at the Spiritualist Church. Before I knew it, they compelled me to go inside. I sat at the back, and as I listened to the service, a feeling of peace and calm swept over me. I felt I had finally come home and that everything would be okay.

I attended the church every Sunday and Monday, and little by little, I felt I was getting my life back on track. I was making new friends and meeting so many people, and the support I received was overwhelming, and for this, I will be forever grateful.

I was twenty-four years old when my journey began, and now, I understand I had to go through the despair, the depression, and even the suicidal thoughts so that I could help others and understand fully what they were going through. I believe they had brought me so low so that the world of the spirit could work with me, pick me up, and make me aware of their presence in my life.

CHAPTER 6

Grandma Lewis

"You won't forget a woman like her, she is a timeless gift, woven into the heart and cherished forever." - Gareth Lewis

Grandma Lewis was a very spiritual woman, as were all her family. When her father passed away, my mum was about three years old. Grandma went with her mother, sister Jenny, and brother Bill, who were incidentally working Mediums, to see a Medium who practised transfiguration to see if he could get in touch with my great-grandfather. As they arrived and knocked on the door of a large Victorian terraced house, the door opened, and they were greeted by the Medium's wife, a polite but sultry-looking lady who invited them in and instructed them to take a seat in the parlour where the reading would take place. They sat in this dimly lit room quietly, not saying a word, squashed together on the settee, with an old, quite tired-looking wing-back chair placed in front of them. The curtains were drawn too, and the fire was blazing. It was time, and so a tall, slim gentleman entered the room. With very few words being exchanged, he settled into his chair to begin.

As the room fell silent, and with a couple of intakes of deep breaths, my grandma saw the Medium's face change into that of her father. Jenny whispered, "Look, it's Dad."

"Shhh," Bill whispered. Energy filled the room, and a thin mist surrounded the Medium, who then spoke, but not in his voice. It had somehow changed, sounding very much like their father's. "Hello," the likeness was uncanny, and for a moment they were taken aback until finally my grandma summoned up the courage to ask, "What's it like, Dad? Are you all right?"

He told them the story of how, at first, he had not realised that he had passed away. He had walked down a country lane. It was unfamiliar, and it confused him how he had arrived there. Ahead of him, there was a crossroads, and standing at it were a group of people. As he walked closer, he realised they were members of his family who had already passed, including John, a child that he and my great-grandma had lost in infancy. He wanted to join them, but they told him, "No, you're not ready yet. You have a task to complete first." Then they pointed down another road and told him this was the route he had to follow. Walking down the lane, he came upon a beautiful little cottage set back in a large garden that was completely overgrown, and he knew at once that he had reached his destination. All of his life, he had lived in little terraced properties, with only a yard at the back, and he had always longed for a house with a garden. My great-grandmother was overcome with emotion and asked, "When can I come and join you?" He replied, "Not yet, Sarah. I'll send for you when the garden is ready." The reading ended, and astounded by what they had just witnessed, they thanked the Medium and left.

The years rolled by, and when my mum was expecting me, her grandmother became very ill, and her mother became increasingly worried about her condition. She rang her sister Jenny to voice concerns over their mother's health, whereupon Jenny told of the dream she had the night before. In her dream, Jenny had found herself on a country lane, and at the end of it stood a little cottage in the grounds of a beautiful garden. She walked up to the garden gate where her father was waiting. "Tell your mother the garden's ready," he said. Later that day, my great-grandmother passed to spirit, and when the story was relayed to me many years later, I knew it was a very significant piece of evidence of what happens to us when we pass.

Over the years, I have heard many stories like this, which makes me believe more than ever, that when we pass to spirit, we will go to our heaven. People ask me all the time, "What heaven is like?" I always answer by saying, "Heaven looks like whatever you want it to look like. You will be where you are the happiest."

Sometime later, Grandma started a job as a housekeeper at the Overdale Training Centre in Bolton. It was a large detached house where young people went for training when they were doing the Duke of Edinburgh Awards. It was a live-in position, so she, Grandad, and Uncle John, who was about eleven, packed up their possessions and moved in. The house was large and roomy and had been through many uses over the years, so it had plenty of character. On one occasion, when Mum went there to visit, Grandma was busy, so she called out to Mum to put the kettle on and said she would be with her in a couple of minutes. However, when Mum got to the kitchen, she found the kettle was already boiling. Not thinking anything of it, she just presumed that Grandma was getting forgetful, until she was told by Uncle John that every time he had a bath, he would go to the bathroom and find that the taps were already running. That was not the only thing that freaked Uncle John out in that house, either. His bedroom was once an office, and one night he was woken to the sound of a typewriter tap, tap, tapping away. Terrified, his eyes scoured the room, and over by the far wall sat a man at a desk. He closed his eyes tightly, and when he opened them again, the man had gone. The encounter made his blood run cold. Uncle

John was extremely psychic, but not knowing at such a young age, it was just a gift he had that ran through our family.

Grandma's job as a housekeeper was always in demand, and after a few years, she moved on to another position as a housekeeper, this time in a bungalow for a company called Magnesium Elektron in Swinton, Manchester. The bungalow was for salespeople and people from other companies who were visiting the site, so they didn't need to stay at a hotel. Her role was to keep house and prepare breakfast, lunch, and evening meals for the visitors. Strangely, some months before, a Romany fortune teller knocked on the door where she was living and mentioned that she would soon live in a bungalow with her family. When she got the job, the local newspaper interviewed her, and she told them about her encounter with the fortune teller, who was spookily accurate.

They had built the bungalow on the site of an old manor house close to the company that employed her, and it was usually busy with people coming to and from work. One day, she was in the house alone. She had just started her day, and there were no visitors on this occasion. As she walked from her quarters at one end of the bungalow to the lounge, which was at the other end, she opened the door to the lounge and could feel a drop in temperature. She paused for a second before she stepped into the room—a room that she had never seen before because it was not the same one that had been there before! This one was styled from an age long gone, and standing at one end, in front of a huge fireplace, were a couple dressed in clothes from the same era that the room belonged to. They turned and saw her standing aghast in the doorway and called out, demanding to know who she was. And as she stepped back in fear, they disappeared.

Spurred into action, she did a bit of research on the original

43

house, so set off to the local library and searched through any books that she could find on the subject. When she got home, however, she felt that the atmosphere in the bungalow had somehow changed and was not now as welcoming as it had been before.

Time went on, and the feeling in the house was becoming more troubling to her and then one night she had gone to bed as usual. Grandad was already asleep, and after a bit of tossing and turning, she drifted off into an uneasy sleep. Suddenly, she was pulled from her slumber by the smell of rotting meat. Her eyes adjusted to the dark, and she could see hams and sides of meat hanging from the ceiling. She gasped in horror when all at once, the stench was replaced by the sweet aroma of fresh herbs. Turning to her husband, who was still fast asleep, she shook him roughly, shouting, "Wake up, wake up!" He grunted and rolled over to look at her. "What? What have you woken me up for?" he demanded. "Look up there," she said, pointing at the ceiling, his eyes following her pointing finger, which stopped at the scene above. Then he rolled back over and said, "I don't know what you're talking about, woman. Go back to sleep; you're just dreaming." She knew that he too had seen the hideous sight but would not admit to it.

A few weeks later, Uncle John came home on leave from the RAF and slept in one of the single rooms. As I have mentioned before, my Uncle John was a very psychic person, so when, one day, he after putting his military boots on top of the dresser and they came hurtling across the room towards him, he wasn't especially surprised. He just calmly said, "Don't throw things at me," and picked the boots up and tucked them under the bed. After several days, the atmosphere in the room was becoming unbearable, and he was getting bombarded by objects thrown at him by unseen hands. These included anything that wasn't nailed to the floor—books, hairbrushes, you name it. They were thrown at him, and he was becoming unsettled and couldn't wait to leave. Meanwhile, Grandma and her assistant were working in the kitchen, the food processor churning away on the kitchen top when their happy mood was shattered as the heavy Kenwood industrial food processor came flying across the kitchen towards them, the cable pulled clean from the socket. Screaming, Grandma pulled her assistant out of the way with not a moment to spare as it crashed to the floor in front of them, leaving them pale with shock and fear.

"Oh my God," she gasped, "that could have killed us," as two of the men staying at the bungalow came running into the kitchen, summoned by the loud crash and the screaming women.

"How on earth have you dropped that?" one man uttered, looking at the object on the floor. "It'll take two of us to lift it."

The two women just looked at each other in silence.

Things came to a head the next night when, once again, my grandparents were in bed having just nodded off after a hard day when Grandma was woken, this time by a hand crawling up the bed towards her. Terrified, she called out, "Paul, Paul." This was not my Grandad's name—he was called Frank—but it woke him up and he pulled himself over towards his wife. He felt the tension in the room, but remaining calm, whispered, "What's the matter? Who were you shouting for?" Silently, she gestured towards the bedspread where the hand had appeared, but which was now replaced by a covering of laurel leaves, which she was later to discover was protection from evil sent from the spirit world.

The next morning, they contacted a Medium to come and

cleanse the house. The Medium, a young lady with long dark hair stretching the length of her back, arrived and knocked on the door. Answering the door, Grandma invited her in and offered her a cup of tea. The Medium, with a calm and quiet voice, politely declined and asked if she could be taken straight to the kitchen.

"Of course," Grandma replied, and they headed off towards the kitchen. As she opened the door, it was not the kitchen that my Grandma worked in, but a room from some bygone day, the atmosphere heavy and threatening. The medium fell into a trance-like state and overshadowing her, my Grandma saw what looked like a holographic image of a masculine-looking woman wearing an apron—the bearer of the hand that had been clawing up the bed the night before. There was a sense of evil about this woman as she raised her arm and pointed towards my Grandma.

"You are the devil's child, she said. "You will bring disrepute on this family, and I will not let you do that."

The Medium turned and headed out of the kitchen towards John's bedroom. She had returned to her normal self by this time and she sat down on the bed, gesturing my Grandma to do the same. She clasped Grandma's hand and said, "The woman we just encountered in the kitchen was the cook to the family who owned the manor house that once stood on this land. When she first saw you, she thought you were the kitchen maid who had worked with her."

She paused as if to catch her thoughts for a moment and then carried on. "The kitchen maid was just a young girl that the son of the house took a fancy to, so he took advantage of her and it wasn't long before the girl became pregnant, his name was Paul." My Grandma whispered, "Yes I've heard that name."

The Medium continued, "The cook was infuriated. She did

46

not blame the son of the house; she blamed the young innocent girl for leading him on, and she feared her employers would blame her for not keeping the girl under control. After all, she oversaw the kitchen staff. So, one night she crept into the girl's bedroom while she slept and strangled her, then carried her outside and threw her body into the river that ran alongside the house. A laurel tree now grows at the point where her body was thrown into the water."

She turned and gazed out of the window for a moment, then turned back and said, "When you showed an interest in the house and investigated, that is when the evil returned. Now, we have to send it back to where it came from. We must pray." Grandma and the Medium sat and prayed together for a while, and then the Medium opened her eyes and said, "I believe that the spirit has gone."

After that, peace returned to the house.

Job made bungalow dream come true

● Mrs Kathleen Lewis outside the bungalow. She and husband Frank live there during the week and at their other home in Bowland Drive, Bolton, at the weekend

STORY BY JOAN SEDDON

SEVEN MONTHS AGO a mysterious gipsy knocked at the door of Kathleen Lewis's home in Montserrat, Bolton.

After asking for the customary palm-crossing with silver she told Mrs Lewis that within six months she would be settled in a lovely bungalow home.

Mrs Lewis lightheartedly took the prediction but thought the woman had merely told her what she wanted to hear.

"I was puzzled how she had read my mind but a bungalow home for my husband and myself had always been my ambition."

But the mystery deepens even further. Within two months Mrs Lewis had taken over the job of housekeeper at the Clifton Junction firm of Magnesium Elektron.

And with the job went the use of a "lovely bungalow home" for herself and her husband.

The bungalow is a little rural and homely oasis in the middle of a desert of imposing and somewhat frightening looking chimneys and industry.

As housekeeper at the bungalow she entertains visiting delegations from as far afield as China and America.

"The visitors from abroad usually come on a short residential basis and other groups for conferences and meetings.

At the "bungalow" there is accommodation for seven people with a conference and banqueting room.

The rooms are also used for anniversary and leaving presentations at the firm.

AWARD SCHEME

Mrs Lewis, well known and loved in the Bolton area for her work at the New Oxendale Training Centre, where she was formerly resident housekeeper, is finding her switch from education to industry a pleasant change.

At New Oxendale, Mrs Lewis was cook, temporary mum, problem-solver, bottle-washer, hostess and instructor all rolled into one.

She catered for huge conferences, taught schoolgirls how to run a home, and trained managers for the Duke of Edinburgh gold award scheme.

At her new job the work is much less emotionally demanding. She has the help of her immediate superior, Mrs Jillah Moran from Clifton, the catering manager for the firm.

"I can turn to Jillah if any problems turn up with which I feel I can't cope."

But how does she cope with a meal for a party of Glasgow industrialists?

"We served them a lovely traditional British meal with roast beef and potatoes as the main course — they seemed delighted with the change" she says with her customary cheerfulness.

She and husband Frank live at the bungalow during the week and then return to their other home in Bolton at the weekend.

"The firm have provided everything for us here. They have been marvellous."

One point which she could find a little disquieting is the bungalow "ghost."

The bungalow was built on the site of the ancient Clifton Hall or Manor House which dates back to the Civil War and before.

Local legend has it that a mysterious spirit from those days walks the bungalow and he footsteps have been heard by both staff and regular residents.

"But whoever he is, he seems to be a friendly spirit," says Mrs Lewis, "the atmosphere in here is too homely and comfortable for him to be anything but."

**Grandma Lewis
Outside the Bungalow**

Grandad Lewis, Mum & Me

CHAPTER 7

Mrs Holden

"In a world of countless faces, there shines one who sparked our change; let us always remember to thank those who inspire us to be better." - Gareth Lewis

When I first attended the Spiritualist Church in Horwich, I was a little nervous as I didn't know anyone there. But it wasn't long before a small elderly lady with short, wavy white hair came across and introduced herself. With a kind smile, she said, "Hello dear, I'm Mrs Holden," in such a gentle voice. I immediately recognised her as the Medium who visited our home all those years before to help my mum with her psychic nights. As I introduced myself, she took my hand and said, "Nice to meet you, dear," and took her seat. After that, she would always seek me out when I went to church, eventually insisting that I sat in the chair next to the one she had been occupying for many a long year. I secretly thought that this was a bit of an honour because she was highly thought of in the church, and no one would have dared to challenge her anyway, as she was a formidable woman. We would sit together and listen to visiting Mediums giving messages to the congregation. Usually, she would sit quietly, taking it all in, but then sometimes she would stare at the Medium, shaking her head and saying under her breath, "No, no," usually when the Medium was struggling to connect to people in the spirit world and was giving psychic messages instead. The first time this happened, she turned to me and said, "Listen Gareth, you must always trust your friends in the world of the spirit. They will never let you down." And she was right; she was always right.

Mrs Holden had been a long-serving member of the Horwich National Spiritualist Church, serving as a committee member, trustee, and even as an ex-president. She was also what I call an old-school Medium, serving local Spiritualists Churches for over forty years. As a well-respected Medium and teacher, she wasn't one to take any nonsense when it came to mediumship. Spiritualism was a very important part of her life; it was a religion she believed in deeply. On the occasions I went to watch her working in the churches, you were not only amazed by the evidence being given from the world of spirit, but you could also feel love from the spirit person in the way she conveyed it.

Some Mediums demonstrate their ability by doing flower readings. This is where you would take a flower to a demonstration, place it on a table, and the Medium gets drawn to a particular flower, forms a connection with the spirit world, and gives the owner of the flower a reading. As Mrs Holden would say about many styles of connecting with spirit, "There's no need for that, dear, they are just playing." When I say this is what she would say, I don't mean privately; she would say it in a loud whisper, and I'm sure the Medium would hear her.

She was not one for not speaking her mind, especially when it came to working with spirit. There are quite a few things I agreed with her about. Take the flower readings, for example. You don't need a flower to connect with the spirit world; this is just a tool being used by the Medium to make that initial psychic link between them and the sitter. People use many tools, cards and crystals, to name a couple. I believe these types of tools will help the Medium and the sitter to focus on something. The real problem, is that it's not being taught correctly.

I wouldn't say for one minute that Mrs Holden was lonely. She would always look forward to Monday evenings of Mediumship at the church, and I think it became more of a social thing and less about receiving a message. She would always introduce herself, as she did with me, to everyone who had never visited the church before and gave them such a warm welcome that the next time they came, they would go straight to her to say hello. As you can probably gather, she was a massive presence in the church. Not everyone liked how outspoken she was, but looking back, that's what I loved about her.

When I first started working as a Medium in different churches, Mrs Holden would ask if she could come to keep me company, and I think she was glad to get out of the house and be in the presence of like-minded people. At first, it was quite nerve-wracking knowing she would be in the audience watching me work and not knowing what she was thinking or even saying to those who sat near her. I say that, but occasionally, I would see her out of the corner of my eye talking to the person sat next to her or even hearing from the platform what she was saying: "No dear," "Not very good tonight, is he?" and things like, "I think I will have a sweet, do you want one?"

It took a while for me to get used to this, and I could then understand how other Mediums would feel when she sat in their audience. I don't think those who sat around her could believe what she was saying, especially when they knew she was with me. I knew her, and knew what she was like, and more importantly, knew why she was doing it. I very quickly got used to it.

What I mean when I say I knew why she was doing it is, this was part of my teachings from her. I mentioned she would keep me company on those sometimes-long journeys, and on the way, we would talk about many things: what we had been doing, what's been going on at church, just idle chit-chat. On the way home, however, our journey was not so enjoyable. I'm not saying this for any bad reason; I just knew as soon as we would pull away, she would say in that softly spoken way, without looking at me, "Well, Dear," and I just knew all the way home she would talk about my work that evening—sometimes harshly, but always her criticism was constructive.

She would always ask me first, "How did you think that went?" This was always a hard question to answer because I didn't know if she would agree or not if I said it was okay. On those journeys home, Mrs Holden would go through every message I'd given that evening and tell me where I had gone wrong and how I could have done better. She was never nasty, just honest and would explain how I could give the message more depth, and how I shouldn't repeat certain words, and a big part of the talks was always my presentation. Sometimes I was relieved when we eventually got back, but I always went home and reflected on what she had said. I learned more on those journeys than I ever did in any circles I had ever sat in.

One night, Mrs Holden and I were invited to perform with another Medium at a charity event at a little church in Cleveleys. and when I say "little church," it really was just that. It had been a house at one time, which had been converted into a church, and I have very fond memories of being there. It was special. We arrived that night and sat on the "stage," which was not a stage at all, as there wasn't enough room. It was in the bay window of what was once the living room. I was feeling very nervous as I had never been to this church before. It was my first charity evening, and it was my first time working with Mrs Holden. The other Medium was doing a flower demonstration! "Well, that's a lot of nonsense. How can you connect with the spirit of a flower?" hissed Mrs Holden in my ear, shaking her head. She then leant forward, staring at a young lady in the front row, and mouthed, "No, dear?" I sank down into my seat as she leaned back and continued shaking her head.

On one occasion, they invited Mrs Holden to be the guest Medium at a church near Blackpool. She asked me if I would drive her to the church for the Sunday divine service. Of course, I said yes; it was not only a way of paying her back for all the teachings she had given me and keeping me company on my trips, but it was also a fantastic opportunity to watch a wonderful Medium at work. On this, what was a miserable Sunday afternoon, I went to pick her up at the arranged time. As we all know, the British love nothing more than talking about the weather, and this was our conversation as we set off. Giving ourselves plenty of time, knowing the church was only forty-five minutes away, I would always drive extra carefully when Mrs Holden was in the car, but the weather was quickly getting worse.

As I got on the motorway, with visibility at a minimum, we changed our conversation to the usual: what we have been doing, church, etc. Just before I was due to come off the motorway at the Blackpool turn-off and driving in the first lane, two cars raced past me, one in the middle lane and the other in the outside lane. I remember saying, "How stupid," and then, within a split second, the car in the outer lane cut in front of the car in the second lane, clipping the front of his car and ultimately colliding with mine, making us spin. We eventually stopped on the hard shoulder, facing in the opposite direction. The other two cars had stopped in the first lane. I immediately turned and said, "Are you OK?" And with a very calm response, she said, "Oh yes, dear, are you?"

They had damaged badly the door and wing on my side, and I was hurting a little. When the police and ambulance arrived, I got out and spoke with them and heard that the other two cars were in a road rage with each other a few minutes before the accident. I couldn't believe what I was hearing—the stupidity of some people, especially when the weather was so bad. Mrs Holden was asked if she wanted to go to the hospital, but she said she was okay, just a little shaken. While we were waiting to be recovered and safely taken off the busy motorway, Mrs Holden was more worried about letting the church down than worrying about whether she was okay. This is the dedication and love she had for the spirit world. Eventually, we got back home. For a lady in her 70s, she never once complained about the accident; she just made her sincere apologies to the church and rebooked a new date.

Over the years, our friendship grew, and I would visit her at home. She was looking after and caring for her son, Peter. Unfortunately, Peter had a major stroke when he was in his early 30s, leaving him paralysed down his right-hand side. Peter needed full-time care, and Mrs Holden, as any mother would, stepped up and cared for him. On my visits, we would sit in the kitchen, and then out came the tea and biscuits as she told me about all the experiences she had as a medium. On one occasion, her story was about physical mediumship, something that is rarely done today as it involves sitting with one person over a length of time. I would love to have experienced some things that she did. She described the time she went to a séance where ectoplasm came off the medium, and the spirit person who manifested through the ectoplasm pointed to Mrs Holden and told her to touch the ectoplasm, describing it as feeling like silk. The spirit world is always present, and the reason she had been asked to touch it was that a few days before, she had been thinking that she would love to know what ectoplasm felt like, and the people in the spirit world had granted her wish.

I was still finding it difficult with my mental health and coming to terms with living by myself. Mrs Holden would always have a small bag of shopping for me. She used to say, "It's not much, but at least I know you have a little something in the cupboards." I would always tell her not to give me anything, but she wouldn't listen. During this period, and with Mrs Holden getting older, she found it more difficult to care for her son Peter, so he had to go into a care home. This upset her, but she knew it was the best thing to do. I would, on occasions, take her to visit him. I think it's fair to say when he moved out, there was a big gap in her life. After all, she had cared for him for many years. Peter sadly died in August 2009, and Mrs Holden was reunited with him just one month later when she sadly passed after a very short illness.

Mrs Florence Holden was an inspirational Medium who was a bit like Marmite—you either liked her, or you didn't. She taught me more than I could ever put into words. She listened to my problems and told me, "If you ask the spirit world, they will always help, even if it's not in the way you were expecting." To this day, when I'm teaching, I always teach the way she taught me.

Throughout this account, I refer to this wonderful lady as 'Mrs Holden' and not Flo or Florence. This is because of the respect I have for her, and even though we were friends, she never asked me to call her by her first name. I'm so privileged not only to have known her, to have been taught by her, but more importantly, to have called her a friend.

Not long after Mrs Holden's passing, I began doing after more teaching and running residential courses, and more recently, online mentorship tuition. As I have recently mentioned, Mrs Holden taught me so much, and now I teach the way she taught me. Some say I have a direct way of teaching—well, that is probably true. Nobody ever blew smoke up my backside. I understand direct teaching isn't for everyone, but all the students I have helped over the years were warned at the start: I won't take any nonsense. I am here only to help you enhance your Mediumship, not to make you look good. You soon find out who wants to learn; those who stay are the ones who can handle being told when they are wrong and can be better. The ones who think they know better and want to be told they are fantastic soon leave.

Mrs Holden

CHAPTER 8

Adele

"Beware of the masks people wear; even shadows can come from light." - Gareth Lewis

Eventually, I got over the trauma of my first disastrous marriage and moved on with my life. I got a new job delivering cars for a hire company, socialised with my friends more, and I really felt happier than I had for a long time. Life as a single man was quite good. I was attending a lot of church services to keep me busy.

It was March 1997; I was twenty-six years old, and I was chairing a service at Horwich Spiritualist Church. As I sat on the stage watching the Medium work, my eyes wandered over the congregation. It was then that I noticed two ladies and a young lady seated between them amidst a sea of faces. I had seen them before, a few weeks previously, when I had been serving the church. Although I had not given them a message, I had noticed them, especially the young lady.

When the service was over, she approached me and asked if I would have a word with her mum, who was sitting with her aunt. Intrigued, I agreed. I approached the two ladies and explained that their daughter had asked me to come over and talk to them. The aunt smiled and gestured for me to sit down. It turned out that her mum was grieving the loss of her son, who had taken his own life earlier that year.

Talking to parents about the loss of a child is incredibly difficult, and I still struggle with it even now. The pain of their intolerable loss is unbearable, and they are often inconsolable. When the child takes their own life, the inevitable question is: why?

This lady was no different. She had so many unanswered questions—why had her son taken his own life? Why she had not seen it coming? How could he do such a thing and leave them all behind with no explanation? The grief was clearly etched on her face. I could easily empathise with this lady as I had contemplated taking my own life only a year or two earlier. As I looked at her, I thought that this could easily have been my mum sitting there, desperately looking for answers where often there are none. I know better than most that depression is an all-consuming thing; you don't think of the repercussions of your actions or of the people you love and who love you that you are leaving behind. You are only looking into that black hole of despair, and sometimes death feels like the only option.

As I sat and listened to her story, I could tell her that her son was now at peace. When he passed over, he would have been met by friends and family members in the spirit world who would take care of him as he transitioned into his new 'life' and that he was doing fine. I could see the relief on her face as she had been suffering from the popular misconception that people who committed suicide were trapped in some kind of limbo, I had heard this so many times before, so I explained to her that if you believe in God, you also believe that He is all-forgiving, and that He loves us, and would never leave us in life or in Spirit. I hoped my words had given her a little comfort, and so I got up to leave to let her think about what I had said.

The next week I was at the church again, and once more I

spotted the three of them sitting in the congregation. When the service was over, the young lady approached me once more and said, "Thank you for talking to my mum last week. You really got through to her. You do not know how much your words have helped her."

"I'm glad I could help," I replied, and with that, she introduced herself as Adele. We got into a brief conversation, realising that we had friends in common. I did not see Adele at church in the following weeks, although her mum and aunt continued to attend. As the weeks turned into months, I thought I would never see her again.

It was on Boxing Day of that year. I visited a local pub with one of my friends, and there she was. I couldn't believe it. Adele was with the girlfriend of one of my other friends, and we quickly got into a conversation. Six months passed, and we were now dating and getting to know one another, Adele moved into my flat, and a couple of months later she told me she was pregnant. It was unplanned and a bit of a shock, but a nice shock, so we made plans for our new arrival. We were both so happy and excited, but alas, it wasn't to be, because at eight weeks of the pregnancy, Adele miscarried. We were overwhelmed by grief and disappointment. Deep down, I felt that the baby would have been a little boy, and I have often wondered over the years how his life would have turned out, and what he would be like now. I will never forget that day. It was November 4th, 1998. Losing a child is difficult enough, but to lose someone you never got to meet is just as difficult. I get asked a lot about what happens to an unborn child when they go to the spirit world. I truly believe that they will be met by family members who have passed before, and their spirit continues to grow, never being far from the loved ones they have left behind in this world, just the same as anyone who passes over.

In February 1999, we put our grief aside a little when Adele became pregnant once more. We were so happy, but a little nervous in the early months. As time went by and we got past the first three months, we could relax a little. We moved out of the flat and rented a house on Watts Street in Horwich. It was only a small two-bedroom terraced house, but it had a small yard at the front and one at the back, giving us more room for our new arrival. It was in October 1999 when we got to welcome our beautiful son Jack into the world. We were a proper family, and I thought my heart would burst with happiness.

Jack was only a couple of months old when I was invited to hold a demonstration at a church in Bury. Adele was excited to come and watch me, so she asked her mum if she would babysit for us as it would be our first night out together since the baby had arrived. Her mum, however, had already made plans for the night, but she said not to worry—she was only visiting a friend, so she would take Jack with her. She was sure her friend 'Janice' would not mind. I was listening in on the conversation as Adele made her plans with her mum, but as soon as I heard the name Janice, my blood ran cold. "Over my dead body, is she taking my son anywhere near that woman?" I declared.

Janice had befriended Adele's mother. I didn't know her, and there was no reason I would want to. I had no interest in her until I discovered she was 'bad-mouthing' me to anyone who would listen, mainly Adele's family. I did not know what I had done to offend her. Janice claimed to be a Medium who was in constant communication with Adele's late brother. I could only assume she was a leech who attached herself to the recently bereaved, vulnerable people who hung on to her every word and believed everything she said in their time of grief.

Unfortunately, there are many such people—so-called Mediums, without the proper knowledge and development, who take advantage of people when they are at their lowest point, not knowing or caring about the damage that they can cause. They also give ammunition to the sceptics and non-believers to fire at genuine Mediums who are following an established religion. I found out that Adele's brother had apparently been talking to Janice daily, and what he was saying about me wasn't nice. I had absolutely no idea why this woman hated me so much; I didn't even know her!

It wasn't long until I found out the reason Janice hated me so much, and the most ludicrous part of the whole sorry scenario was that it wasn't even me who she was angry with. Who, you may ask, had ruffled her feathers so badly? Well, it was none other than my dear old dad! This was the man who had abandoned me and my brother, and left my mum to look after us on her own, and now I was being targeted because of something he had done! And what major crime had he committed against her? Well, I'll tell you—it was because Janice was a member of a group that was trying to get greyhound racing banned, and my dad was deeply involved in greyhound racing; it was his passion. In Janice's mind, the apple doesn't fall far from the tree!

So back to the story at hand—after I had told Adele in no uncertain terms that Jack was going nowhere near Janice, she phoned her mum back to cancel the babysitting and told her the reason. Her mum was obviously upset by this, and it caused Adele and I to argue. I left the house under a cloud and headed off to my demonstration, feeling a bit annoyed and upset. I didn't want to upset my wife or her mum, but I had to protect my son. Despite the upset at home, the demonstration of Mediumship went well, and I had a brilliant night. It couldn't have gone better, and I came out of the church on cloud nine. I felt as if people in the spirit world had taken all the hurt and anger away and replaced it with a feeling of euphoria. I felt so uplifted as I walked towards my car, but this feeling didn't last long because just as I got into the car, my phone rang. It was Adele. I didn't even have time to say hello before she exclaimed, "Gareth, please, you need to come home now.

"Mum and Janice have been round to the house."

"What happened? Are you okay?" I asked, scared by the tone of her voice.

"Just get home," she said, "I'll tell you then. Hurry Gareth, please."

My mind went into overdrive as I drove home. What could have made her so upset?

When I finally arrived back home, my mind was racing, and Adele told me what had happened. I had trouble containing the fury that was building up inside me as she recounted the events of that evening. Adele explained that her Mum and Janice had visited, knowing she was home alone with Jack. Janice had become like a woman possessed, shouting and ranting about me, accusing me of being controlling and manipulative, and how she knew exactly what was going on. Adele was obviously taken aback by the woman's outburst and gasped, "What on earth are you talking about? There's nothing going on." Janice's face turned purple with rage, and she screeched, "We all know he's physically abusive towards you, and if you don't get out of this relationship now, his anger will turn on the baby! I'm warning you; you must leave him now."

Adele looked at her in horror and uttered, "Are you completely insane? Gareth? Abusive? Don't be so ridiculous." It was then that Adele's mother piped up, "Please listen to her,

Adele. Janice has been in contact with your brother, and he told her everything that's been going on. If you won't listen to us, listen to your brother!" Adele told me she didn't know whether to laugh or cry, but the look on her Mum's face stopped her from doing either. The poor woman had obviously been brainwashed and believed every vile lie that Janice was feeding her.

I was stunned by what I was hearing and all I could say was, "Who is this woman? Why is she trying to destroy us?" "Well, that's not the worst of it," Adele said and continued to recount the evenings events. It unfolded that Adele had sat down on the arm of the chair as she was holding Jack and he was getting fractious with all the shouting and screeching that was going on, and as she looked up to reply to her Mum's outburst, Janice lunged forwards and slapped her so hard across the face that she nearly fell off the chair shouting, "Wake up you stupid girl!" Adele rocked back with the force of the blow, shocked and horrified that not only was she physically assaulted in her own home whilst holding our newborn son, but also that her mother had stood back and let it happen! "Right, that's it," I said, "I'm calling the Police."

The Police arrived and took our statements. We didn't really know much about Janice, other than that she was a friend of Adele's mum, but when we described her to the police, surprise, surprise—they already knew who she was. When she was eventually tracked down, they gave her a serious talking-to and issued a police caution. But it didn't weaken the hold she had over Adele's mum. This caused a massive rift in the family, as Janice's manipulation and control over Adele's mum became evident. She was accusing me of being the very thing she was— abusive and violent. Janice had proven this by assaulting Adele. Although we knew it was grief that bound Adele's mum to this woman, we had to take a step back from that side of the family, which made things very awkward, especially for Adele.

I tell the story as a cautionary tale of how vulnerable people can be taken in by so-called 'Mediums' who have no connection to the spirit world and who are in it to feed off the bereaved.

Two years had passed since this incident, and we had little contact with Adele's mum. Adele became pregnant again, which was a wonderful surprise for both of us, and our second son, James, was born in September 2001. Life went on, and we were content with our little family, but peace would not reign for long in the Lewis family.

When Jack was four years old, Adele woke me up in the middle of the night. "Gareth, Gareth," she hissed, "sort Jack out. I can hear him playing with toys in his room." With that, she turned over and went back to sleep. "Charming," I thought, but I shook the sleep off and slowly got out of bed to investigate. As I approached his room, I could hear cars rolling around the room, and the sound of the police siren was undeniable. I pushed the door open, ready to put him back to bed, but I was stopped in my tracks. Both boys were fast asleep. I rubbed the sleep from my eyes and looked around, and yes, every toy that I had carefully packed into the toy box earlier was now strewn across the floor. Suddenly, a huge energy hit me, and a ball rolled from the corner of the room and stopped at my feet. Now you're probably thinking, "You're a Medium, you deal with spirits all the time, you can't be frightened, can you?" Well, the answer to that is, hell yes. I can be scared, especially by physical phenomena. I remember thinking, "Here we go," as a police car, siren blazing, raced across the floor towards my feet. I jumped away just in time, and the car skidded into the skirting board behind me. I was suddenly aware of the spirit of a child, and with my heart thumping, I said, "Right, you can stop that now, you're going to wake up Jack and James. It's bedtime, not playtime, but thank you for visiting us." I closed my eyes and said a prayer, and I could feel the energy leave the room. All the little one wanted was to be acknowledged, so I checked the boys were OK and scurried back to bed. And I don't mind telling you, I pulled the duvet over my head when I got there!

Over the following months, more strange happenings occurred, and Jack was also sensing spirit. One spirit was a little lady who would hold Jack's hand while he chatted incessantly to her. He would insist that we set her a place at the table and seem to hang on her every word. I couldn't sense her, but I believe she was just a spirit person he was aware of. Some would call this an imaginary friend. I believe that the reason that children are more sensitive to the spiritual world than adults is because they are innocent and see things as they are rather than seeing things as they are told to. In those early years, it became part of our everyday life for similar spiritual experiences to occur. I guess we all just got used to it.

One night, we were watching television when we suddenly heard a dragging, banging noise coming from the bedroom above. As I have already said, we were getting used to these strange occurrences, but it was different this time, as the energy in the house had become heavy. I climbed the stairs with trepidation, and as I reached the top, the energy in the house felt oppressive. I entered my bedroom, and I could feel it at its worst. Sitting on the bed, I closed my eyes and tried to clear it, but it became heavier. I lay back on the bed and rested my head against the pillows when suddenly I felt paralysed as though a ton of weight was on top of me, holding me down. I told myself not to panic, even though all I could feel was raw fear. I could feel the veins in my neck bulge as I struggled for breath. "Please Spirit, help me," I thought, and the weight lifted just enough for me to stamp my foot on the floor to get Adele's attention. I could hear her feet on the stairs as she came to see what was going on, but she seemed to take an age to reach the top. I turned my eyes towards the open door and could see her shadow slowly moving along the landing as though I was watching a film running in slow motion, but finally, she appeared in the doorway, and the weight eased a little more. "Gareth," she whispered, "Are you okay?" I could tell by the look on her face that she was shocked by my appearance. She later told me I looked like someone else, but luckily for me, she knew what was happening and came to sit by me on the bed. I had been overwhelmed by a presence, and Adele knew she had to just be calm as she held my hand and spoke to me gently, telling me to relax. As she did, I could feel the weight lifting and my breathing eased until finally it was gone. It was one of the most terrifying things we had ever encountered. I just hope I never have to go through it again! To this day, I don't know who or what it was. Maybe I had gone into an altered state, and a spirit person had overshadowed me?

Although my spiritual life was a big part of those years, we also had a normal family life. Work was getting busier, and we had an active social life with our neighbours. We would have street barbecues and gatherings—it was a happy time.

In 2007, we had a night out with the neighbours, and it was then that we were introduced to a young woman with long blonde hair called 'Donna'. She was a friend of one of the neighbours and seemed nice enough. We got on well and soon became friends. Adele and I had been thinking of moving out of Watt Street around this time as the house was small and we wanted a garden for the boys to play in, so in December 2007, we moved into a bigger house on Poplar Avenue in Horwich, the same street my flat was on before Jack was born. It had a nice garden and plenty of room for our growing family. I knew Donna had been having problems at home, so when Adele suggested to me she move in with us for a while, I agreed as I thought we would help each other out. We would give her somewhere to stay, and she would help us financially and keep Adele company in the evenings while I was out at work. It was the worst decision I ever made!

Donna moved in, and it wasn't long before the problems started. You would think I would have learned from my experience with lodgers, wouldn't you? But no, apparently not. She was young and single with no children or responsibilities, and she had a great social life. Consequently, Adele wanted to be like that too. She wanted to be out every weekend, and if we couldn't afford it—which we couldn't with two small children and a mortgage—then she borrowed the money off someone else and went out anyway. We argued about this constantly to no avail, and the cracks in our marriage grew.

I got suspicious about their 'friendship,' It all seemed very intense, and I felt like the third wheel in my home. We couldn't do anything or go anywhere without Donna being involved, and she had become snappy and irritated with me. I would ask a simple question like "What's for tea?" and before Adele could answer, she would pipe up, "I'm ordering takeaway for us and the boys—you sort yourself out." Or she would bring sweets and treats in for herself, Adele, and the boys, and they would all sit munching away in front of me, never offering to share. Yes, I was slowly getting the message, but this was my family and my house. I needed to act fast!

I called my friend Diddy. I needed to talk to someone about

all that was going on, and we met at the pub. The first thing he asked as he sat down at the table was, "What's up?" He could see by my face something was wrong, so I told him everything, and he told me to leave. I looked at him in misery and said that I wanted to, but I wasn't leaving my boys. "Look, mate," he said, "Do you really want to live your life like this? Adele is putting this woman before her family and especially before you, so tell her to get out and take her mate with her. That's what I'd do." I took a sip of my pint and said, "That's probably what she wants me to do." I looked up at his puzzled expression. "What do you mean?" he said. "Come on, mate, you can tell me." Slowly, the words fell from my lips, "I think they're having an affair." His face was blank, so I continued, "I think my wife is having an affair... with Donna." Diddy had just taken a mouthful of beer, and when I said that he nearly choked. "You're joking?" he said, aghast. I shook my head, and he said, "Leave." We continued to chat for a while, and then I left. On the way home, I decided I would get Adele alone and confront her!

The next day, while Donna was at work, I asked Adele straight out if she was having an affair, and without a moment of hesitation or regret, she admitted she was 'in love' with Donna and that she was leaving me so that they could be together. Once again, I had been betrayed by the person who I loved, and my world crumbled.

I told her to pack her bags and get out, but she wouldn't be taking our children—they would stay with me. She left for a few days but then came back, to give our relationship another go for the sake of Jack and James. I let her come back because I still loved her and hoped we could make a go of it. We booked a holiday as a family to work things out. We agreed it would be nice to take the boys to Florida. They were so excited and couldn't wait. Everything seemed fine for a while, but just three months later, and two months before we were due to go on holiday, she announced she couldn't live without Donna and she was leaving for good this time. It devastated—not only for myself but also for our children, who would be heartbroken. The 'best bit' of the whole thing came later when she informed me she still wanted to come on holiday with us, so I had to endure the most uncomfortable two weeks of my life, playing happy families in Disney, surrounded by hundreds of other happy families enjoying themselves.

After we got back, I settled into life as a single dad. The boys found it difficult to adjust to life without their mum being around all the time, and it was especially difficult for little James, who couldn't understand why his family had been torn apart. So, for the next year or two, I pulled away from doing the church services which were such an important part of my life. Although I honoured the ones that were already booked and took the boys along with me as we had no babysitter, my relationship with their mum was strained.

Adele moved into her new home with Donna, and the boys stayed with them on Wednesdays and every other Saturday. I was struggling emotionally, and I believe I was on the verge of another breakdown, but this time it was different. I had my boys, especially Jack, who was my rock. He was so strong for me and his little brother, and although he was only nine years old, he was the one who held us all together while dealing with his own upset. I am so proud of you, Jack!

Life as a single parent is difficult, as many of you will know, and you certainly find out who your friends are. I lost so many of my 'friends' after my marriage breakdown simply because I had no partner and could no longer be part of the couple's scene. And because I had no babysitter and couldn't go out every weekend to socialise, I was further isolated. On the weekends the boys were with their mum, James often wanted to come home and be with me. I realised that this was my life, and I had to get on with it. But in the evenings, when the boys were in bed, the feelings of loneliness were overwhelming. This time, however, I knew I had to concentrate on being a full-time dad and that my children would always come first.

CHAPTER 9

The Green-Eyed Monster

"An envious person sees the world through a lens of scarcity, mistaking another's success as a threat rather than inspiration." - Gareth Lewis

As we all know, no matter which path you take in life, there is always the chance of the old green-eyed monster raising its ugly head, and this is precisely what happened to me. Now, you may think to yourself that things like that couldn't happen in a religious setting because Spiritualism is a religion just like any other, but yes, sadly, it can—more often than you would care to know. All it takes is for one individual to feel that their nose has been pushed out, and they will go all out to ruin not just their rival's career but their entire life.

I had been working as a Medium for a couple of years when I met a man who I will refer to as Mike, even though that is not his real name. He was a member of a church committee and would come and sit in a circle when I and my friend John Harrop would visit the church he attended.

John and I became friends just a couple of years previously when I was giving a service at Bolton Spiritualist Church. From that day, we became very good friends and worked together frequently. I still, to this day, consider him to be a very close friend who has always been there for me.

Over time, John and I became friendly with Mike, and he

would invite us to his home to sit for Spirit. In fact, over the next few years, we became good friends. Mike would come and watch John and me when we were doing demonstrations, either together or on our own. It was at this time that I would recommend Mike to the churches I worked in as a new working Medium, to help him start his own journey in mediumship and introduce him to other Mediums to help him get more work. I enjoyed helping others, including Mike, to develop their gifts, but I had my work commitments to honour and also a growing family to support, so our friendship drifted a little as I had become increasingly busy travelling to London and other venues away from my locality. It was at this time that I heard from the churches I had recommended Mike to that he was rude and cutting in the way he was conducting himself on the platform. Although I found it hard to believe at first, I had no option but to stop recommending him, as the complaints were rolling in daily.

Life went on as normal for a while, with me travelling around the country until one day, just after I had been on a trip to London, I got a call from one of the local churches cancelling a demonstration that I was scheduled to do. The excuse was flimsy in retrospect—a double booking or something along those lines—but I had no reason to question it. My workload was still heavy, so I put it to the back of my mind until other churches cancelled as well. As the year drew to a close, I noticed that my bookings for the following year were half of what I had just worked, and that was a worry because I did not know why. The New Year came, and after a couple of months, I went to see my friend John to tell him my worries over the sudden lack of work and not knowing why this was happening to me. John went quiet for a moment, his eyes closed in concentration, and when finally he looked up at me, my world was rocked to its very foundation.

"Gareth," he said, "You are being attacked by someone who is out to ruin you." The shock of his words made my blood run cold. I did not know who would do such a thing, but I was about to find out.

A couple of weeks after my meeting with John, and with his words still playing heavily on my mind, I went to watch a demonstration at a church that had been a great supporter of mine; I say "previously" because they were one of the churches who had cancelled on me. It was here that I finally learned the horrible truth.

Walking into the church, I looked around to find the best place to sit, and as I took my seat, the president of the church came hurrying towards me. "Oh Gareth," she said, "I thought you had stopped being a Medium." I looked at her aghast. "Why on earth would you think that?" I spluttered. Her eyes dropped to the floor, and her face turned crimson. What she said next made my heart stop in my chest. "Look, Gareth, I've known you for years," she stuttered, awkwardly fumbling with the chain around her neck," and I don't believe it, but... there is a rumour going around about you." She bit her lip and stumbled on, "They say that you beat your wife and abuse your kids, but I don't know who started it." Her mouth snapped shut, and her lips formed a thin line as she once again looked down at the floor. I stared at her for a moment, not believing what I had just been told. As the tears filled my eyes, I said, "Well, as you have known me for years, and if, as you say, you could never believe such a vile pack of lies about me, then why did you not tell me the moment you heard it? And why did you stop booking me? Because that, to me, just tells the world that you believe it." "I don't believe it Gareth. I'm sorry," she whispered. I got up from my seat and walked out with as much dignity as I could muster.

The journey home was like an awakening, the accusation swimming round in my head. Who could have been so evil and hated me so much to say such disgusting things, especially about my children, who were—and still are—my world? Arriving home, I stumbled into the kitchen and blurted everything I had just heard to my wife, and when I had finished, we just stood in silence and stared at each other, both shocked to the core that anyone could be so cruel to make up such horrendous lies about my family when I didn't even know what I had done to warrant it.

The months went by, and we were still in the dark about who was trying to ruin not just my career but also my life with the evil accusations that were going around. But there was one thing that I was sure of—it was obviously someone from the Spiritualist community, and that hurt the most. One night, my wife and I were invited to a function at a social club in Horwich, and it was there that we found out the source of the lies. My wife had gone alone as we couldn't get a babysitter, and I had gladly stayed at home as I wasn't in the mood for socialising. A couple of hours had passed, and I was sitting in front of the TV when the phone rang. I dragged myself up from the sofa to answer it, and what I heard turned my world upside down. It was my wife who was calling, and as her story unfolded, I had to sink down onto the stairs to stop myself from falling. She had discovered who had started the vile rumours that had ruined my life.

My wife had been enjoying her night out, chatting with friends and relaxing with a drink, when she paid a visit to the ladies. She went through the door and was immediately followed in by a lady who she didn't know but who was desperate to get her attention. "Excuse me, love, can I have a word?" My wife turned, wondering what the stranger wanted. "Look, you don't know me," the woman continued, "but I know Gareth, and I have just heard something that has sickened me to the core." That got my wife's attention, and she took a deep breath and waited for what was to come. The woman launched into her story, saying she had been sitting at a table with a so-called Medium—her words, not mine—who was full of his own self-importance, bragging about how gifted he was. But when he turned in his chair and pointed at my wife, she really pricked up her ears because she knew who I was and that this was my wife who was being pointed at. "See her over there," he slurred to the group, "that's Gareth Lewis' wife. He's a Medium too, and he abuses his own kids!" The lady was totally shocked at what she had just heard. She knew me and told my wife that this person was spreading disgusting lies, and when she had seen my wife going into the ladies, she had run after her because she thought we should know what was being said. My wife ran out of the toilets to confront him, but the snake had got wind that he had been rumbled and had slithered away. And the name of the vile, lying snake? MIKE.

Yes, Mike, the person who I and my good friend John had given so much help and support to, who we had introduced to churches, who we had spent so much of our time helping to develop—not only had he tried and nearly ruined my professional life, but worse, the injury and hurt that he caused my family, especially my children, is totally unforgivable.

I hope that one day he gets to read this book, because although I have changed his name, he will recognise himself, and I hope he hangs his head in shame, although I know he probably won't. People like him don't have a conscience, do they? Ironically, after not seeing sight nor sound of Mike since he was outed at the social club so many years ago, he has recently emerged from under his stone into a house just up the road from where I live. I see him most days walking his dog past my house, but his head is always down, and he never makes eye contact, so maybe he has a conscience after all!

The news eventually spread about the lies and the betrayal, and the churches that had hurt me so much by choosing to justify this terrible lie and cancelling all my work tried to get in touch and book me again. The damage was done, and I never worked at any of them again and I never will. Although, through this, I have been taught a hard lesson and that is not to trust people too easily. I also know that people like this are in the minority, and it has not diminished my love of the Spiritualist Church or of the good people within it.

CHAPTER 10

Coronation Street

"Some people enter your life like quiet whispers, yet unknowingly, they shape the direction of your future with profound impact." - Gareth Lewis

In mid-1999, I was working as a car valet for a dealership in Bolton. I gained as much experience as I could, and in early 2000, I set up my valeting business with a friend of mine. He saw an advert for someone selling a fully equipped mobile valeting van with the possibility of taking over the work he did for the popular television series *Coronation Street*. We quickly bought the van and any work that came with it, including the work at *Coronation Street*. After a quick chat with the head of security and a background check on us, we secured the deal, and they gave us our security passes so we could enter the studios.

Unfortunately, the partnership only lasted a few months as he didn't think there would be enough work to pay us both a decent wage, and he was right. Setting up any business is hard, but I will give it a go, so I bought his share and continued by myself.

The work was difficult, and sometimes I couldn't work because of the bad weather. It had to be terrible weather to prevent me from working as I had a small family to look after. Anyway, I was used to working outside after all those years working on the markets. As well as building the business with private work and car dealers, I was getting to know the cast and crew. My regular day there was Thursday. I would turn up in my little van, and after a time, the security guys saw my van approaching and knew it was me, so with a quick flash of my card, they would let me through.

It always surprised me every time I arrived at the studio, there would always be a regular group of people waiting to see if they could spot one of the cast members from the soap and the waiting press, especially if there was some gossip going around. I was often asked if I knew if a certain celebrity was there. I would never answer, but they would always ask, often and even going to extreme lengths, including climbing trees near where I was parked or shouting through the gates behind me. It just made me laugh. I would keep my mouth shut because I really enjoyed working there.

I would pull up at the end of the car park and set up my van for the day. The cast and crew would give me their keys and tell me what they wanted doing. As time went on and I became more and more known by everyone, I would often sit in the tearoom with the cast and talk with them. I couldn't believe I was sitting with the actors from a show I had grown up watching. I would clean the cars for most of the cast, and they would always find time for a quick chat. I remember thinking the only person I hadn't spoken with was the longest-serving actor on the show, William Roache, who played the character Ken Barlow. I would see him park his car, and he always said 'good morning' or 'hello'. I didn't clean his car or know him well enough to approach him. To be honest, I was a little star-struck by him, being one character I had always seen on television from being young.

I would look forward to Thursdays, knowing I was going to

'the street' and not knowing who I was going to see. I think I was becoming one of those fans I would see at the gates of the studio, but I was allowed in.

One Thursday afternoon, whilst waiting for someone wanting their car cleaned, I noticed a lad named Chris making his way over to me. I knew him as one of the crew, but he was wearing a *'Stars in Their Eyes'* sweater. This was a show that was filmed at the same studios as *Coronation Street*. I said 'hi' to him, and he told me he was working on *'Stars in Their Eyes'* that week, and they were filming the grand finale. For those who don't remember *'Stars in Their Eyes,'* it was a show where people would come on the show and then transform into a famous singer and perform like them. Chris said, "I'm glad you're here. Do you want to come and help film a promo for the final?" "If I don't have to sing, yeah, why not," I replied and followed him over to the studio where it was being filmed.

As I walked onto the set, I saw a group of people standing around a red carpet. I was told I was going to be someone from the press and was given a camera and an overcoat. Then I was told to pretend to take photographs when directed. So off I went to the red carpet, and out of nowhere, the host of the programme appeared and stood next to me. Oh, my goodness, I thought, it's Matthew Kelly, and he was huge! I'm 6ft2 and didn't realise how tall he was from seeing him on television. I looked up and said 'hi' in a shy voice. With that famous smile, he asked how I was. Before I could answer, it was time. The Director shouted, 'places everyone' and 'Action!' Matthew introduced the programme, and I pretended to take pictures of him. Within moments, and after just one take, my television debut was over. On the evening it was due to air, I told everyone, and a couple of friends visited to watch with me. Within a flash, there I was, and everyone around me shouting, "Is that it?" but inside I felt like a star!

One Sunday evening, I was doing a divine service at Congleton Spiritualist Church, and after the service, whilst having my coffee, I saw a poster on the notice board with a picture of William Roache on it. I rushed over to see why he was on the notice board in a church. Unbeknown to me, he was a very spiritual man and was giving talks about his own spiritual beliefs. And he was going to be at that church the following month. I knew I couldn't attend that night because of another appointment, but I was intrigued to know more and had the perfect opportunity to talk to him directly, but I had never really spoken to him. That following Thursday, I was going to pluck up the courage and introduce myself.

I had been at the studios for about an hour and could see William's car wasn't there, not knowing if he was going to be in or not, when suddenly I saw his car pull up. As he got out of his car and made his way to the green room, I went to approach him, but my nerves got the better of me. Later that afternoon, I was on my way to the tearoom for a drink. As I passed the dressing rooms, there he was in front of me. Nervously, I said, "Excuse me, Mr Roache." He turned and with a warm smile said, "Hello, you're the Valet." "Yes," I replied, "sorry to bother you. My name's Gareth," and I went on to say how I saw his poster in church. "Oh yes, do you go to the church?" he said. I explained I am a Medium and served the church at the weekends. His face lit up. "Really?" he said. "Look, I just have to go into the studio. Will you still be here this afternoon?" Playing it cool, I replied, "I should be, yes" "Great, well if you are, come to my dressing room, say about two p.m.?" With a smile and a nod, I said "OK," and off he went. I couldn't wait and didn't really want to clean any cars, but I knew I had to, so I could be free that afternoon.

Two o'clock came, and I made my way down the corridor to William Roache's dressing room. I couldn't believe it. I knocked on the door, and he welcomed me in. We sat talking about our beliefs, and what his talks were about, and he asked me about being a Medium. That was the start of our friendship. Whenever I was there, we would often meet up and have a chat about all kinds of things. I found him not only nice to talk to but very intelligent in all things spiritual.

I had been working for *Coronation Street for* a good few years now, and occasionally, I had to take my boys, Jack and James, with me to work. They were only seven and five years old. Nobody minded me taking them along. They would just sit in the van playing their games or sometimes playing football with the younger members of the cast. On this particular day, I was busy working and William Roache pulled up in his car and asked if I had time to clean it, which I did. He noticed my boys sitting in the van looking bored, so he offered to take them on a private tour of the street and inside the studios. They jumped at the chance, especially Jack, who was doing a little acting in short films himself. So off they went, and again, I was just amazed that someone so famous would take the time to do that, but I knew he had a very kind heart, unlike some celebrities I've met.

An hour later, I met up with them as they were making their way out of the studio. William had given them both a little gift. I don't think they still have it, but Jack remembers him doing so. In those eight or nine years working at Granada Studios, I appeared on 'the street' a few times, driving my little van and meeting a lot of actors who visited the studios. There was one occasion when William introduced me to a very respected and well-known Medium by the name of Gordon Smith, a Scottish

Medium who was going to be in Manchester. William had arranged a private reading with him and would I like to go along. Again, I jumped at the chance. I couldn't believe I was going to meet a Medium who I had so much respect for.

William met me at the hotel where Gordon was staying, and he would introduce me after his reading. As I waited for him to arrive, I was sitting in this five-star hotel thinking, "Wow, I've never been in a five-star hotel before!" I'm easily pleased, I know. When I'm on the road, I stay in some 'lovely B&Bs,' never a five-star hotel. William arrived, and we went and waited for Gordon in the bar area. Within a few minutes, Gordon called William to follow him to his room for the reading. As I waited, feeling a mixture of excitement and nerves, I kept looking around the room, not feeling like I fitted in. After an hour, William and Gordon returned to the bar area, and I was introduced to Gordon. William said his goodbyes as he had to go back to work, and Gordon led me to his room for a chat.

We sat and talked for a while, and he said he didn't think he had a reading for me when I instantly jumped in and said, "That is not why I am here, it was just nice to meet you." He said, "No, there is a reason we have met, and I think I know what it is." "OK," I said, looking confused. "Have you ever been to the S.A.G.B (Spiritualists' Association of Great Britain)?" he asked. The S.A.G.B is in Belgrave Square, in a very nice area of London. The building was a very old Victorian-style building where they conduct workshops, evenings of mediumship, etc., and it's known worldwide for hosting some of the best Mediums. I replied, "Never, but of course, I had heard of it." "Leave it with me," he said, "and I will put your name forward."

Thanking Gordon for his referral and endorsement, I gave him my details and, in a state of shock, I left. I remember thinking on the way home how someone of his stature was going to recommend me.

Within a couple of days, they booked me to work at the S.A.G.B in London the following year. I only went a few times and eventually declined an invitation to return as this was at the period of my life when I was having problems at home, and I didn't want to be away for weeks at a time. If it hadn't been for William Roache, I would never have met Gordon, who I still know and have contact with, and feel privileged to say I have worked at the S.A.G.B.

During that time, William and I visited churches together, where he would give his talk, and I would then do a demonstration. When William came up with the idea, I had mentioned to him I was talking to a church, and they asked if I would ask him if he would go there and give one of his talks. Of course, he said yes, and suggested that I do a demonstration straight after him. I agreed and contacted the church to confirm our booking. As we arrived, the local papers got wind that he was going to be there, and after a quick chat with their reporters, we headed into the church and were guided into the Mediums' room. As William was the first to speak, I left him to have a few moments and took my seat in the front row. I was so nervous as I sat listening to him talk. I knew I could just sit and listen to him all day, but I also knew I was due to get up soon. After he had finished, there was a round of applause, and I was invited up to give a demonstration of mediumship. William went and sat at the back of the church, as I knew he was only going to stay for twenty minutes as he had another engagement to go to, but wanted to see me work. As soon as I put my nerves to one side, the demonstration went well, and knowing William had to leave halfway through, I was just honoured to be able to say I had done it. We did a few more of these events over the next few months.

About a year later, I didn't go to Granada Studios much, as many of my regulars had left the show, and the younger and newer actors were not using my services. It was a shame. I have very fond memories of working at *Coronation Street* and, of course, not only to meeting but working with William Roache and being able to call him a friend. It's strange how things just happen in life. Call it fate, coincidence, or interventions by the spirit world. If my friend had not asked me to join him in this business, I would never have had these experiences and met those I did, opening doors and opportunities for me. I will always thank William and Gordon for opening those doors for me.

"I have such fond memories of our meeting with Bill Roache and it's wonderful to see how Gareth and his mediumship has blossomed."

Gordon Smith

CHAPTER 11

Kelly

"You are my best friend, my confidant—together, we are an
unbreakable bond of trust, love, and endless understanding."
- Gareth Lewis

I had been single for about two years when I felt it would be nice to meet someone new and move on with my life. I felt I was getting into a rut, and although the boys had settled into the dynamics of our family life now that their mother no longer lived with us, I wanted someone nearer my age for conversation, companionship and, who knows, whatever else that came along with it.

2011 dawned, and I got the strongest feeling that someone new was going to come into my life. The feeling was so intense that I convinced myself that it was going to happen, but as the year rolled on, I thought maybe I was wrong. August arrived, and I received an email from a lady requesting a Tarot card reading. Nothing unusual in that, only she finished her message with, "P.S. I think we live in the same street." Now, that piqued my interest. I've lived in Horwich all my life and mostly in the place where I live currently, and I pride myself that I know most people around the area, but this lady didn't ring any bells with me, which only made me more intrigued.

The weekend before the reading was booked, I had made plans to visit my friend Craig and his family, who had moved to

Bedford as his wife, Jo, wanted to be closer to her family. I was looking forward to the trip as I had not seen them for a while, and since I had a radio interview in London that weekend, I thought I could kill two birds with one stone. The weekend progressed, and we were having a great time, so when Craig asked me to stay over until Monday, I was tempted. But, I had that reading booked, and I didn't like to cancel appointments. Besides, I was intrigued to find out who the lady was, who had been praying on my mind since I had received her email. So, I reluctantly declined his kind offer and went home on Sunday as originally planned.

Monday dawned, and I started the day as usual. The boys were off school, so I got them ready to go to my mum's and then got on with my daily chores. I was just taking the ironing upstairs when I glanced out of the window and saw a young woman walk past with a young girl. I had never seen her before, so I stopped to look for a moment, and then she was gone. I carried on with what I was doing and waited for my mystery lady to arrive.

A knock on the door jolted me out of my meditation as I prepared myself for my appointment, and my heart quickened as the mystery was about to be solved. I opened the door and was momentarily taken aback because there was the lady who had walked past earlier with the young girl. Still hazy from my meditation, I gathered my thoughts together, and invited her in, and took her through to the kitchen, where I had set out my Tarot cards in preparation. We sat down, and I picked up the cards and shuffled them, then handed them to her to do the same, all the while hoping that she would not notice my demeanour.

It was strange—I felt distracted and excited at the same time. I had worked with beautiful women before, but none that made me feel like this. When she smiled at me, I felt my cheeks flush! "Oh God," I thought, "get a grip, she'll think I'm an idiot." I took a deep breath and asked her to pass me the cards. I laid them down on the table in a spread, and as I did, it became increasingly clear that I was seeing myself in her present and, more importantly, in her future. I panicked, I couldn't tell her; she'd think I was mad or worse. The panic rose, and I had to think fast, so I gave her a reading, trying not to mention her love life. I think I told her she would meet someone soon and left it at that. It's not often that I get psychic evidence in readings about myself, but my overwhelming feeling was that my future partner was sitting in front of me, and the confirmation of that which I saw in her cards was just too good to be true!

I remember I went for a reading once a few years before, where the Tarot reader had told me I would meet a girl of mixed race. It confused me at the time because I was still happily married, so I thought nothing about it until that moment— because there she was, sitting in my kitchen. I hoped she hadn't noticed that I had bumbled my way through her reading like an embarrassed schoolboy. I gathered up the cards and told her I wasn't charging her for the reading as I wasn't happy with it, but she insisted on paying. After the reading, we sat and chatted for a while, and she told me she had her own Tarot cards but had to use a book to interpret the meanings. My heart leapt in my chest—this was it, this was my opportunity to see her again—so I quickly offered to teach her how to read the cards properly, and much to my delight, she agreed.

Over the next few weeks, we got on brilliantly, and as the weeks turned into months, our friendship progressed into a relationship. Eventually, Kelly and her daughter Lauren moved in with us, and she has been a constant support to me in my life and work as a Medium. I felt comfortable going out to demonstrations in the evenings, knowing that my boys were being looked after by someone who I could trust, and this meant that I could resume my career as a full-time Medium. During the day, I, in turn, supported Kelly by doing the school run with Lauren and the boys so that Kelly could train to be an embalmer, a career she had always wanted to pursue. We were a family (though she never learned to read the Tarot cards properly).

Reading the Tarot cards has always been an interest of mine, knowing you can receive so much information from the pictures and words. I always said that creating my own deck was something I would love to do. During the period of COVID-19, with the world locked down and not much you can do to fill your days, I followed that dream and created my own cards. My Silhouette Oracle cards, unlike Tarot, are more Affirmation Oracle Cards, designed to encourage positive thinking and self-confidence, as well as unlock your intuitive gifts. At the time, I had a student, Lisa Cole, a very talented artist who helped with the design of my cards by creating the artwork through the technique of encaustic painting, also known as hot wax painting. I then included my spirit-inspired words to match each card.

CHAPTER 12

Ouija

"The Ouija may bridge the gap between worlds, but it may also open doors that are best left closed." - Gareth Lewis

The Ouija board, also known as The Spirit Board or The Talking Board, is one of many tools that can be used to contact the spirit world. The name "Ouija Board" is a trademark created by the manufacturer of the 'game,' Hasbro Inc. The word "Ouija" is derived from the French and German words for "yes." The board is marked with the letters of the alphabet formed in an arc across the middle, with numbers 0 to 9 underneath in a straight line. The words "Yes" and "No" are placed in the top left and right corners of the board. The 'game' is played using a planchette, which can be made from either wood or plastic, to spell out the messages from the other side. In my opinion, this is a waste of time because if someone from the spirit world trying to get a message across, they wouldn't need fingers on planchettes; they would move it themselves.

Ouija Board's, as most people already know, can be made from pieces of paper and an upturned tumbler and there are many people who have entertained themselves by pushing an upturned tumbler across the dining table at social gatherings. Ouija Board's, if used correctly, can be a good tool for communicating with the spirit world, but I would never recommend or encourage anyone to use one, especially if they are inexperienced. The reason is that they can channel terrible energy or negative entities if not controlled or handled with care.

My first experience with an Ouija Board happened when I was about ten years old, near the flats where I lived. My friends and I were out playing near some garages that people used to rent out, as we had no drives or garages of our own. Suddenly, a young teenage boy, who in retrospect I can now describe as being in a psychotic state, ran past us, tearing his hair and emitting a terrible screeching sound. He was pursued by two more teenagers who seemed to be trying to catch him to calm him down, giggling nervously as they ran past and out of sight. I looked at my friend, and shrugged my shoulders, and we got on with our game. Later that day, while chatting with some older boys, I mentioned what I had seen earlier. They told me that the lads in question had been going into the garages all week to play with an Ouija Board, I didn't know what an Ouija Board was back then but didn't want to show my ignorance, so I kept quiet and just listened to their tale. Their story was that day they had finally got a result, so to speak, and a man from the spirit world came through, and told the terrified teen that he was going to kill him. This explained why the boy had been so scared, especially as the entity was pursuing him down the road and right past me. Listening to these words made my blood run cold.

It wasn't until many years later, as an adult, that I fully understood the effects of the Ouija Board and the serious implications of using them. Over the years, people seeking help have approached me many times after using the Ouija Board. Sometimes it's just a case of people giving themselves the jitters, but then other times it's not so simple. On one occasion, I was waiting for a gentleman to come to my home for a reading when I was overcome by a sense of foreboding. In fact, from the moment he rang me to book an appointment, I felt uneasy, and as the moment of his arrival approached, the feeling of dread intensified. For a moment, I was on the point of cancelling his booking, but then I realised it would be unfair to cancel at such short notice. When the doorbell rang and as I got up to open it, all my feeling and insight of the spirit world shut down. It was almost as if the Spirit world had put up a big metal shutter. I opened the door and blurted out, "I'm sorry, but I can't let you come into my house!" He looked at me and asked, "Can you tell me why I can't come in?" I replied. "It's because I feel that you have been dabbling with a Ouija Board, and I'm sorry, but I can't help you." He put his hand to his head, and nodded in agreement, and muttered that he understood. I felt so bad as he turned and walked away, because I knew he was terrified and didn't know what to do, but I was relieved that he hadn't come into my house because I was just not strong enough to deal with such powerful energies. I believe that those in the Spirit world didn't want me to try.

On another occasion, a young man came to see me for a reading. It wasn't until he sat down that I got an uneasy feeling that something was not quite right with him. As I started his reading, I soon realised just how troubled he was, and the reason was that he had been playing with an Ouija Board. I told him I could not help him, because, once again, the metal shutter had been pulled down by those in the spirit world. However, I told him I would not charge him anything. He looked up at me with troubled eyes, and it was then that he blurted out the events that had led him to seek help.

After spending a year at university, the young man and his girlfriend had taken a gap year to travel around Australia, where they had a wonderful time taking in the sights and soaking up the sun. Their trip was ending when they booked into an apartment where they met up with a group of people who introduced them to the Ouija Board. It all started out as a bit of fun, sitting around, getting drunk, and playing the board. At first, there were no major happenings, just a slamming door, and the odd candle being snuffed out, but nothing major. The weeks rolled by, and one evening, when his girlfriend was out working in the local bar; he had an early night and went to bed. He was just drifting off to sleep when there was a sharp tug at the bedsheets. His heart jumped, but there was nothing there, and he drifted back into a light slumber. Suddenly, he was pulled back to consciousness when the sheets were yanked completely off the bed. Terrified, he ran from the bedroom and sought sanctuary in the lounge in front of the television, waiting for his girlfriend to return from work.

When she arrived home, he blurted his tale out to her, but she just laughed it off and said that he was probably just dreaming and not to drink so much when he was home alone, although he hadn't been drinking that night. Time passed and more things happened, but only when he was home alone—a glass was smashed against the bedroom wall, the television switched itself on, and one night he was woken by the smell of smoke so strong that he thought the house was on fire. It dawned on him that all this weird stuff had happened since they had been messing with the Ouija Board, and he knew he had to get rid of it as the friends had moved on and left it behind in the house. That night, when his girlfriend had left for work, he took the board, put it into the outside bin, and went to bed reassured that his troubles were now over. He was, however, woken when his girlfriend returned from work and she came into the bedroom saying, 'And you wonder why you freak yourself out?' He rubbed the sleep from his eyes and asked her what she was talking about. She beckoned him into the lounge and pointed to the coffee table where, in pride of place, was the Ouija Board. Blood pounding and heart thumping, he grabbed the board, took it outside, and burned it, convinced that this would solve the problem once and for all. He was tired of constantly being woken in the night, terrified of what would happen next, and not only that, but his girlfriend was also being dismissive and accusing him of being neurotic.

Things came to a head when phenomena happened when his girlfriend was home. She had witnessed nothing before, but when the bedsheets were snatched off the bed one night when she was there, enough was enough. They cut their trip short and come home. Once back in England, they decided he would go back to his flat, and his girlfriend would return to her parents' home. He was so relieved to be back in familiar surroundings and looked forward to some undisturbed night's sleep. That night, he went to bed happy, but the happiness didn't last as he soon realised that whatever was haunting him in Australia had followed him home and was now here with him in his flat. As he drifted off to sleep, he felt something grab his ankles and drag him off the bed. Terrified, he spent the rest of the night in his car. The next day, he phoned his girlfriend and invited her over to stay the night. He omitted to tell her the events of the previous night, but as soon as she arrived, she felt uneasy. That night, when she had gone to bed alone, he said that he would follow her shortly. After a few minutes, he heard her scream and ran to the bedroom to find her sitting in the corner, crying and shaking hysterically, screaming that she had just been dragged out of bed. He had to tell her then that he suspected that whatever had terrorised them in Australia was now here in his flat. She couldn't believe that he had brought her to his flat knowing that the 'thing' was now here and with that, she grabbed her things and left, ending their relationship.

His story told, he shrank down into his chair; his despair was clear to see, and I felt desperately sorry for him, but there was nothing I could do for him. I know it sounds awful, but I just wanted to get him out of my house. I excused myself and went into the kitchen, where my partner was waiting for me to finish my readings. And I quickly told her the story and that although I wanted to help him, I just had no clue what to do. Kelly, my partner, had been raised Roman Catholic, and she immediately said to tell him to see a priest, as they would know how to advise him. She was so convinced that I went and relayed this advice to the young man, who was just grateful to be given some hope. I bid him goodbye, relieved that he was out of my home, and set about burning sage to cleanse the house. I often think of this young man and hope he got the help he needed.

CHAPTER 13

The curse

"Hell is empty, and all the devils are here."
- William Shakespeare

I used to believe that 'cursing' was a nasty, flippant comment people used to throw around to frighten each other, you know, the classic, 'I curse you' scenario. Well, I don't think that now because I have come to know that thoughts are living things. Words and negativity can be directed towards another person, resulting in negative situations arising around them.

One day, I was doing a reading for a lady. She had an air of sophistication around her and was very quietly spoken. I took her into my living room, and as she settled on the sofa, I could see that her eyes were filled with sorrow. Within seconds, I could sense the energy in the room begin to change, becoming aware of two people from the spirit world, and the overwhelming feeling of such a wealth of love, touching my aura. It was then I knew I had her husband and their son wanting to communicate with this lady. As I was explaining to her what I was feeling and who was coming through, her eyes began to well up with tears. "Your husband and son both passed very suddenly and both unexpectedly," I explained. "That's correct," she replied. "Your husband is making me aware that it was just over a year after his passing when your son sadly passed, and he needs you to know he was there to meet him when he passed over." As the tears began to roll down her face, she reached for the tissues in her handbag and replied in a broken voice, "Yes, you are correct. My son passed a year after I lost my husband. Thank you; I am so glad to know they are together. You don't understand how much that means to me, just to know his dad was there for him when he passed."

It was at that point that I got a very strong feeling that there were a lot of negative people around her who, for whatever reason, were being nasty about her and talking behind her back. 'Do you feel that you are being attacked in some way?' I asked. She replied with no hesitation, 'Yes, I am being attacked.' I had a feeling that there were two people causing her such a bad time, and I found it very hard to understand why anyone could be so cruel, especially after everything that she had been through. I decided to push the feeling aside and carried on with her reading. I went on to explain that they would both be with her later that afternoon when she went to place flowers at his graveside, as it was the anniversary of his passing. I also described how her husband was such a caring family man and loved her so much, ending the reading with him saying, "Gareth, please tell her I will help her through the situation that is making her feel like she is being attacked." "I do hope so," she said.

She then sat back in her seat and told me the reason why she thought she was being attacked. She told me that she was Jewish and that in her culture it was possible to verbally curse someone to do them harm. She went on to recite a saying by Rabbi Geoffrey Dennis, which stated, 'In Jewish thought and text, curses amplify the belief that speech can have tremendous power.' Continuing her story, she told me that she had suspicions that her family was being cursed, which had started before her husband's death when their business had run into difficulty. They were struggling financially after previously doing so well, and for no apparent reason other than bad luck, her husband had then tragically died, leaving her to raise their thirteen-year-old son alone. She felt that no one could be so unfortunate.

Getting on with her life for the sake of her son was now her main concern, and she was fortunate to have the help of her best friend and her husband, who were supportive and helped her through the most difficult period after her husband's death. She even felt that without them, she would never have coped and was so grateful for their help. Tragedy was to strike again in the cruellest way when her now fourteen-year-old son was killed by a car on his way home from school. My heart went out to her; she had suffered so much in such a short space of time. She took a deep breath as if to compose herself and then said, "My entire family was gone, and it was then that I knew for sure that I had been cursed!"

Her friends, who had been so supportive of her when her husband had died, were there again, offering help and advice and were of great comfort to her as she had no one else in the world to turn to. But after a few weeks, she started to notice that things were going missing from her home, and she decided to confide in her friend that she thought she had been the victim of a curse. "Why on earth would anyone want to curse you?" her friend had exclaimed. She went on to tell her about all the things that had been taken—things of great sentimental value but of no value to anyone else. "Look," her friend responded, "You are still grieving; maybe you just moved them somewhere without realising." But she was adamant that this was not the case, that she knew someone was attacking her, and whoever it was had access to her house. So together, they came up with the idea to make a list of all the people with keys to the house—parents, in-laws, a friend, and her husband, and finally a cleaner who she had known for ten years. Immediately, the friend pounced on the cleaner as the guilty party. The lady paused and looked up at me, "I knew that it wasn't her Gareth," she said. "I had been friends with my cleaner for over ten years, and she loved my son. She would never do anything to hurt us, not by words or actions." She dabbed her eyes and got back to her story. After telling her friend that there was no way it could have been the cleaner, the friend got up to leave, telling her to think long and hard about who could have been to blame and that she still thought that it had to be the cleaner.

After the friend had left, she sat and stared at the fireplace, thinking of who would want to harm her and not coming to any conclusion when something caught her eye. She sat up and saw that there was a space where her heart-shaped crystal paperweight had been, and what's more, she knew it had been there earlier because she had picked it up to watch the light catch it when she had been dusting. Realisation dawned with such heart-breaking force that she had to catch her breath because she now knew that the person who she had loved as a friend, who she thought had loved her and her family too, was indeed the one who was trying to destroy her. She just didn't know why. Later that day, after mulling things over, she decided that she had to find out for sure, and so sent her friend a text message saying that she needed a change of scenery and would it be all right if she visited their house this Saturday for a change instead of them coming to her. They responded that yes, that would be fine, and so the scene was set.

Saturday arrived, and she went to the friend's house as planned. After a bit of pleasant chatter, the friend said that she had to just nip out to the shop for some milk, and as the friend's husband was at work, she was left alone in the house.It was too good an opportunity to miss, and she set about looking around to see if any of her missing ornaments were there. Climbing the stairs, she had an overwhelming urge to look in the back bedroom, and when she opened the door, the first thing, she saw was the paperweight sparkling on the window ledge. Before she could go any further, she heard a key in the lock of the front door. Closing the bedroom door as quietly as she could, she rushed downstairs to find the friend's husband standing in the hallway. She rushed past him, saying she was sorry but that she had to leave as she felt unwell, which was not entirely a lie because she felt sick to her stomach that she now had the proof that the people she had known and loved for all these years were the ones who had destroyed her life. After that day, she cut off all contact with these people, and they obviously knew why. But she never learned the reason why they had turned against her and her family, and she probably never would. I still question to this day whether the couple who she considered as friends were taking her personal items to use in some kind of black magic or dark witchcraft, or whether they were manipulating her into believing that she was cursed and had some spiritual attachment that was causing chaos in her life. I don't know—maybe they were just thieves.

CHAPTER 14

The Voodoo Man

"Guide me to see what's hidden, for I can't solve what I can't find." – Gareth Lewis

Like many other people, I used to think that Voodoo was a bit of nonsense—people cursing each other, dressing up, and chopping chickens' heads; you know, the things you see in horror films and not much else. But I was wrong. Voodoo is a religion. Like Spiritualism, people who believe in Voodoo believe in two worlds: death being a transition into a world we cannot see, where our ancestors watch over and inspire us. There are great variations within Voodoo beliefs and practices, as with everything, where there is good, there is always going to be bad. I had given little thought to Voodoo until the day when an African man came to my house for a reading.

The man was very polite and friendly, but as soon as I started his reading, I knew that there was a darkness around him. Before I could stop myself, I asked him if someone he knew had been dabbling in Voodoo. Where this thought came to me from, I don't know, but he nodded his head and quietly answered, "Yes." I told him I was aware of a young man of his acquaintance who had been knocked off a bicycle and killed. Once again, he just answered, "Yes." I looked at him. His eyes were downcast, his hands clasped. "Are you questioning if this was an accident or whether Voodoo caused it?" I asked. He lifted his gaze and looked into my eyes. He replied "Yes, that is correct!" Suddenly, a block came down, and I couldn't proceed. I explained that I didn't feel comfortable any more as there was a dark, negative presence around him, and that I wouldn't be charging him for the reading. His shoulders slumped in disappointment, but he was understanding, if not a little surprised at my honesty. He asked me if I would like to hear his story, and I agreed.

Back in his homeland, Africa, his family had been having some problems with another family, and he was suspicious that Voodoo was involved, as his family were experiencing some horrible things. After a while, he distanced himself and came to England to start a new life. However, things did not improve, and negativity continued to follow him, including the death of the young man on the bike. He told me that all he wanted was to know if he was correct in his assumption that he was being attacked by Voodoo. I felt uneasy as I watched him. He was sweating profusely and wringing his hands, so I told him I was sorry that I couldn't help him but that I knew someone who could. My friend, John Harrop in Manchester might perform a cleansing ritual on him if he wished, and he quickly agreed. I phoned John, who agreed to help, and when I went back into the room to tell him the man, he was so grateful that he insisted on paying me in full, although I told him it was unnecessary.

The following week, I had a booking from another African gentleman who also wanted to know if he was under the influence of Voodoo magic. I had a feeling that they were acquainted, so I gave him John's number, and he went on his way. A few passed, when I knew there was a dark cloud over my home. My partner and I were bickering over trivia matters, work dried up for both of us, we were struggling financially, and the children were frightened to go to the bathroom at night because they could see dark shadows on the landing. My partner, Kelly, struggled with controlling her diabetes, and her health was suffering; we dreaded being in the house at all. To add insult to injury, the front of the house got 'egged' by kids—or so we thought. The final straw came when Kelly, feeling unwell, went to lie down in her daughter's bedroom. Her head was thumping, so she opened the window as wide as it could and fell asleep. After an hour, she was abruptly woken by what she thought was my voice, and as she rolled over, she thought she saw me standing over her, watching her sleep. It was only as she rubbed her eyes that she realised I wasn't there. Jumping off the bed, she rushed downstairs to find me working on the computer in the kitchen with the door shut, "Have you been upstairs?" she asked. I replied that I had been working in the kitchen since she went for a nap because I didn't want to disturb her. At that point, we decided that we too needed help from my friend John, so I phoned him straight away.

A few days later, I went to collect John. I hadn't told him much of what had been going on, just that we needed a cleansing in the house. John walked through the kitchen and said that he couldn't feel anything, but when we got to the living room, he sat down and exclaimed, "Oh yes, he's here, he's dark, and he's African!" Sitting down across from him, we told him of all the strange and scary events of the last few days, and when we mentioned the 'egging' to the house, he said that one of the African guys who had come to him for a clearing had told him that throwing eggs was a way to curse someone—you curse the egg and the throw it at the victim's house, "Oh, God," I said, "And we thought it was just kids messing around."

"Well, maybe it was," John said, gazing round the room, and then he stood up and said, "Right, let's get started."

Lighting sage and letting it burn until it created a thick smoke, John walked from room to room, shutting the doors and windows as he went and 'smudging,' the energy of the house. When he entered Kelly's daughter Lauren's room, he said, "Oh, he likes it in here," and he stayed longer in the room, paying more attention, allowing the smoke to fill every corner of the room before closing the door. By the time, the house was by this time filled with white smoke, and John advised us to leave it for a while, so we all went out for curry. When we returned a couple of hours later, John told us to open all the doors and meet him back in the kitchen. He then opened the back door wide, and all I can describe it as was a whirlwind of smoke being sucked out of the house. "There he goes," John said, and after twenty minutes, the house felt light and airy, and the children were no longer afraid.

Over the years, I have learned that the mind is a powerful tool and that you don't have to be a follower of Witchcraft or Voodoo to curse someone. Anyone can do it; you just have to have the mindset and the belief that it will work—and it probably will!

CHAPTER 15

The Medium and the Alien

"Life's funniest people are the natural comedians, these people have a God-given gift to make people smile and cry with laughter, without realising what they have said or done."
- Gareth Lewis

Over the years, I have met some extremely interesting characters. Some of them make me smile, others make me cry, and then there are those who make me want to hide my face in my hands from sheer frustration. Although Mediums share the same fundamental beliefs, there are different aspects to mediumship that I do not believe in. In this chapter, I am going to relate to you some of my most memorable moments, from the alien communicators to the healer who thought it appropriate to share his wife's most intimate female problems.

There are many ways in which Mediums work to communicate with Spirit. Some work in an altered state using their senses—hearing, seeing, and sensing—which in spirituality is known as Clairaudience, Clairvoyance, or Clairsentient. Others work through the Trance Mediumship, which is when the Medium allows a person in the spirit world to draw very close, overshadowing them, and allowing their voice box to be used as a means of communication.

Alien communication! Now that's one I'd never even heard of, well, at least not in a Spiritualist context, until I was invited to a demonstration where the Medium claimed to do just that! To say that it intrigued me is an understatement, and I couldn't wait to hear what he had to say. The event was by invitation only, a closed circle, and there were about twenty of us who had been invited to witness the demonstration. The atmosphere was somewhat hushed, and eyes were darting around the room, not quite making contact, as though everyone was a little nervous about what they were about to witness. The hall was dimly lit, and you could have heard a pin drop as the Medium went into a trance, allowing the 'alien' to communicate through him.

The voice of the 'alien' was not much different from his own, but I must be honest—he caught my interest as he described the planet from which he came. After a while, he asked if anyone would like to ask questions. A lady sitting to my right asked, "What is the name of your planet?" A reasonable question, I thought. "The planets where I am from do not have names because they are hundreds of light-years away," was his reply. What was I hearing? I couldn't believe my ears. The planets have no names because they are hundreds of light years away? Well, how do you explain why our planets all have names when they are hundreds of light-years away from you? It felt like he was put on the spot and couldn't make something up quickly enough, but I bit my tongue and kept quiet. The next question came from a bemused-looking chap, "Do you visit us a lot?" "People from my planet are around you every day; you are just unaware," was his reply. Well, I can't prove he was making it up, but let's just say it wasn't very convincing.

Moving along to the end of his demonstration, he gave out information to individual members of the circle, I being one of the honoured few. He told me that in a previous life, I had been one of the Twelve Disciples and that because of this, I had great healing powers. He failed to tell me which one of them I had been, and it was too late to ask because he had moved on to the chap next to me, where he announced, "And you, sir, were Jesus Christ himself." I turned to look at the man involved, who had a look of surprised disbelief on his face, and I couldn't stop the smile that tugged at the corner of my mouth. I came away from the evening feeling more amused than educated. Can we communicate with aliens? Who knows!

Over the years, I have worked with many different audiences. Some people just come to watch while they are socialising and out for a drink; others are desperate to know what the future holds for them. Some people who attend have a genuine interest in the afterlife, and then there are those who come to cause trouble and ruin the night for everyone else, probably because they don't understand, are afraid, or are just plain ignorant.

One evening, it was the 'just plain ignorant' who I encountered. There were three of them sitting around a table, and they were intent on causing trouble from the start. As soon as I came on the stage, they began talking in overly loud voices—so loud that it was difficult to make myself heard. People were turning around in their seats and shushing them, but this only seemed to inflame the situation. Eventually, a member of the management team went over and told them to be quiet or leave. This worked for a while until I reached the questions and answers section of my demonstration, and then it all started again. One of the trio stood up and asked, "When did you first realise that you could do this?" So, I explained about my experiences throughout my life, from childhood through to the present day, but this did not satisfy them. Another of the group stood up and shouted, "What a load of rubbish, you haven't answered the question!" I was taken aback because I had clearly answered the question, and it baffled me about their aggressive attitude.

It was then that another member of the audience, who was clearly getting fed up with the antics of the trio, stood up and shouted, "That's enough! Why don't you shut up and let him get on? You're ruining the night for everyone!" Before I knew it, the whole audience had turned on the three troublemakers, shouting at them to shut up and leave until they eventually did. But it was no use—the energy in the room had gone, and I had to wind up the demonstration with no one getting a message from their loved ones. I apologised to everyone as their evening had been ruined, but they were fine about it and understood that it wasn't my fault. Although I remember that night for the troublemakers, I also remember it for the kindness of most of the people there.

Luckily for me, episodes like that are few and far between, and not all demonstrations are heavy with emotion from the relatives of the deceased. Sometimes they are filled with laughter, and since laughter can be a great source of healing, there can never be too much of it for me.

One such demonstration took place at a Psychic Club in Lancashire. I had just finished my demonstration and had sat down to listen to their healing list, which was being read out by a gentleman called Arthur. As he got to the end of the list, he looked up and told everyone that he would like to add his wife's name to the list, as she had been suffering from some intimate health issues. Well, that got my attention and everyone else's too. We all sat up in our seats, eyes forward, mouths open. Did he just say that? Clearly oblivious to the shock on people's faces, he carried on: "My wife is Japanese, and for the last few weeks, she has been suffering from a terrible vaginal discharge which has a terrible odour, so I would ask you all to send her healing thoughts, thank you." One woman at the front looked like she was going to faint, and others, gasping with shock and disdain, grabbed their belongings and made a dash for the door. As I looked around the hall, there was a table of about six young ladies who could not hide their glee, and they were crying with laughter—one of them taking on a resemblance to Alice Cooper. There was so much mascara running down her face. That was enough for me. The pent-up laughter I had been suppressing came bursting out, and I had to lean over and pretend to be searching in my bag in an attempt to hide my hilarity. It did not end there as he just carried right on, "I took her to the doctors, and they said she has something called BV," at this point one of the young ladies was taking a sip of her drink and couldn't help but spurt it out as she tried not to laugh. "I don't know what that means," he continued, "but it can't be good, so I thought I would ask for some healing." That was it! I could hardly breathe, and everyone who had not already run for the doors was either dabbing their eyes or covering their faces completely. Oblivious to everyone's reaction,, Arthur continued to end the meeting with the healing prayer, but nobody was listening. I would normally have stayed behind for a cup of tea, but not on this occasion. I couldn't get out of there fast enough, and I had to sit in my car and compose myself for at least ten minutes before I could drive home.

CHAPTER 16

Reincarnation

*"Reincarnation is the soul's way of gathering wisdom, each life
a new chapter in the endless story of becoming."*
- Gareth Lewis

One of the most popular questions I get asked is, "Do you believe in reincarnation?" And I give the same answer every time: "If there is such a thing, knowing my luck, I will come back as myself," followed by "Well, it hasn't yet been proved or disproved to me." So, what are people's views on reincarnation, and what is it?

Over the years, many people have come to me for private readings, leaving lasting impressions on me. They have made me realise that although many of us have been through tough times that have changed our lives forever, some have endured much tougher times than most of us could ever imagine. I feel overwhelmed by the tragedies of the people I meet. I will never forget them; their courage and tenacity will be imprinted on my mind forever, either through the strength they possess or by the situations they have had no choice but to endure.

I met a couple who came to me for a private reading, and the moment I opened the door to them, I knew they were in trouble. I felt their despair, and it was all-consuming. I took them into my sitting room, and as they sat down, I was immediately aware of the presence of a young child. The lady looked up at me and said,

"You will have to excuse us; this is all very new to us." I told her not to worry and explained to them, as I do to everyone who comes to me for a reading, just to answer yes or more importantly no to any of the information that I give to them. They looked at me and nodded, and so I began.

I told them I was aware of the spirit of a little boy, around about three or four years of age, who was new to the spirit world and had only passed to the spirit world within the last year. It was also clear to me that the child had been struck down by an illness before he passed. Finding it difficult to hold back the tears, the couple nodded. I explained how he used to love playing football in the garden with his dad. At this point, the gentleman couldn't hold back any longer and cried as he held on to his wife. The emotion I felt from him was pure grief. His wife explained that whenever they had the opportunity, they would be outside together, playing with the ball. I continued with the information about how their son had passed. "He is telling me he went to bed that night perfectly fine and woke during the night with a high temperature and crying." The couple, still visibly upset, just nodded. I went on to tell them that by the time he had got to the hospital, he was unconscious and passed away a couple of days later.

The reading had opened wounds that were still very raw for the couple. "Do you have any questions?" I asked. The man wiped his eyes and said, "You know he is still with us, don't you? We feel his presence every day. What I want to know is, when he is reincarnated, will he come back to us?" His wife interrupted, "We are Hindus, and we believe in the soul's reincarnation. We believe our souls will be reborn many times until we are good enough or perfect enough to progress to the next spiritual level." I explained to her that before today, I had given little thought to reincarnation, as I had always believed in the soul's incarnation, in that, we pass to spirit and learn and grow in the world of spirit. "What if you are an evil person, though?" the gentleman asked. "What are your beliefs about that? We believe in karma." I gathered my thoughts for a moment and then I told them I believed that the world of spirit had many levels and that if you were a good person and lived a good life, then you would go to a high level. On the other hand, if you had lived an evil life, you would go to a low level, and there are many other levels in between. Whichever one your soul is assigned to, you will learn and, over time, progress to a higher level. The man looked at me and said, "So if we try for another baby, it won't be him. Is that what you believe?" Not wanting to upset them further or challenge their beliefs, I said, "This is my belief, not anything I have been told to believe by the Spiritualist Church or anyone else; it's just that at this moment, reincarnation has not been proven to me."

They said that they respected my opinion, and then the lady said, "Can I ask you one more thing?" "Of course," I replied. She took a deep breath, then said, "Let's just say that what you believe is true, that our son will not be reborn to us... will he be upset if we have another child? Will he feel betrayed and forgotten? Because he will never be forgotten, and we don't want him to feel that way." I looked into her eyes and saw a sea of hurt and pain. I gently told her that the answer to her question was no, he won't be upset or envious, and he certainly won't feel that he is being replaced, because these are human emotions. When we are in the spirit world, in our spirit form, there is only love—no jealousy, no hate, no upset, just peace and understanding. They thanked me for connecting with their son and took their leave.

This is an example of how I try not to push my beliefs onto

others. Everyone has their own beliefs, and it is not up to me to change them. All I can do is give them evidence that the soul lives on, that the physical body is a shell, nothing more, and that spirit will grow once it has passed to our eternal home. I must admit, though, that after my meeting with this couple, I thought, what if this existence that we are currently in is purgatory? What if we had to keep coming back to rectify past life mistakes... what if this is Hell? As I said before... it's yet to be proven to me!

In the mid-80s, my mum and her friend went to a Mind, Body, Spirit Fayre in Preston. The main reason for going was she heard that there was going to be a gentleman there who was supposed to be a very good Medium. I think, like many people, we think we just need a good reading if for no other reason than a bit of guidance. This Medium was highly recommended and not too far away. She felt it was the right time. On arrival, she saw a poster advertising a talk and demonstration of past life regression in the main hall at twelve p.m. Mum immediately said to her friend, "I would love to be regressed. Shall we stay and watch?" Her friend replied, "Yeah, why not". So, they went in search of the Medium they wanted a reading from. Whilst walking around, Mum saw the gentleman who was going to do the past life regression demonstration.

Never being one for being backward at coming forwards, Mum made a beeline for him. After introducing herself and asking a little about what he would be doing, she blurted out, "Can I have it done on me" Her friend put her head in her hands, saying, "You must forgive my friend. She's not shy." The man replied, "No, it's fine. I'm used to it," and laughed. "Come along at twelve o'clock," he said, "and we will see," and off he went.

After having a lovely reading with the Medium they wanted

to see, they had fifteen minutes until the past life talk, so they went straight to the hall to get front-row seats. The gentleman came on stage, and with only about fifteen people there to watch, he explained what he did and how it worked. Then the time came that my mum was waiting for, and he asked if anyone would like to be regressed. As quick as a flash, her hand shot up. He picked just four people, and Mum was one of them. She and the others took their place on the stage. He walked down the line, gently talking to them and using the techniques he uses to place them in that trance-like state of hypnosis. Unfortunately, two of the four didn't respond and asked to leave the stage, leaving Mum and another lady. After trying with the other lady and realising she wasn't completely in that altered state, he saw my Mum was and focussed on her. He began by telling Mum, "You are safe, you are okay, just keep listening to my voice." He then went on by telling her to go into a tunnel whilst assuring her she was safe and well. When he felt the time was right, he asked her to come out of the tunnel. He then asked, "Where are you?"

"At home with my mum" she replied.

"What are you doing?"

"Having my dinner."

"What are you eating?"

"Chipssss" she replied.

"Do you like chips?"

"Oh yes!"

Later, Mum was told by her friend that all her answers were given all the way through in a little girl's voice and with childish expressions.

The gentleman then told Mum to go back into the tunnel, still telling her she was safe and to listen to his voice. "Where are you now?" he asked.

"I'm in the classroom at school."

"Who's your teacher?"

"Mrs Phoenix," she replied.

"Do you like your teacher?"

"Not really. When you don't do as you're told, she pokes you in the back and it hurts."

Mum then added what the school looked like and described playing in the playground. With this, he then asked for her to go back into the tunnel, still assuring her she was safe.

"Now, come out of the tunnel and tell me where you are."

"I'm in a building, in a big house."

"And what are you doing?"

And at this point, Mum started to cry.

"Why are you crying?" he asked, still in a childish way. "I shouldn't be here. That's why I'm hiding."

"Why are you hiding?"

"I can see them burning people."

"Burning people?" he asked in a puzzled voice.

Getting quite upset and crying, she replied, "I can see them burning people. They are witches, and they are burning them." And explaining how she could smell the smoke in the room as the witches burned. Realising she was getting quite upset and bothered by what she was seeing, she was then asked to go back into the tunnel where she would be safe, and no harm would come to her. Again, he told her just to listen to his voice and assured her she would be okay.

Once more, he asked, "Where are you now?"

Again, as a child and always a little girl, she replied, "I'm at the market square, watching the horses and carts and the beautiful ladies with their long, flowing skirts. They have aprons on carrying baskets full of fruit and veg to sell."

He then asked, "What are you doing?"

"Thank you," she said, "That lady has just given me an apple."

"What can you see now?"

Laughing like a little girl with her hand over her mouth, she said, "I'm at the side of the river," and pointed.

"What are you pointing at?" he asked.

"I'm not telling you."

"Why?"

Still giggling like a little girl, she said, "It's that little boy over there. He is weeing in the river."

He then asked, "What's your name?"

"I'm not telling you!"

"Why?"

"I'm not telling you."

"Okay, well, how old are you?"

"I'm not telling you."

And with not getting any more information about the little girl, she was asked to walk on a little further and explain what she could see.

"I'm walking down the streets."

"What's the name of the street?"

"There is no name. Oh, look at that; there's a man," and without saying she just mimed a man juggling.

"Oh, look, there is a man with a stick. It's on fire, and he's putting it in his mouth." Describing a small fairground going on around her on this market day, the gentleman then asked Mum to go back into the tunnel, assuring her she was safe and that everything was okay. She was then brought back into the hall. On opening her eyes, she couldn't believe that the audience, which began with around fifteen people, had grown into a full

116

room, with people standing at the doors watching what was going on. Mum was asked if she was okay, and with that, she left the stage to a round of applause.

On the drive back, her friend told her what she had witnessed and couldn't believe how her mannerisms had changed and how much she was crying all the time, convinced Mum was just a little girl. On reflection, Mum came away feeling that she had been through a mind-blowing experience. This is something Mum has never forgotten and remembers as vividly as she did just after it had happened. She explains it as if the back part of her brain was totally with him, and the front part of her brain was still in the room.

My only personal experience of having a past life regression was in the late 1990s. I was invited to a private gathering of invited guests only at my church in Horwich. It was a warm Saturday afternoon, and when I turned up, there were about ten of us sitting in a semi-circle facing three chairs. As we sat there waiting for the gentleman, who was also a wonderful Medium, to come and take the session, everyone was sat talking about who they might have been in a previous life. While I was there with an open mind, I didn't really know what was about to happen and if I really had been here before.

The gentleman came in from the back of the church, accompanied by the President of the church. They took their seats facing the semi-circle, with the President sitting to his left, leaving the chair to his right empty, ready for one of us to take and be regressed. Frequently, in a Spiritualist Church, before starting any service or event, we began with the President giving an opening prayer. This is so important as we ask for protection and guidance, if nothing else. So, as the prayer ended, they introduced the gentleman to us, and you could feel the tension rising in anticipation of what was going to happen. He stood up and spoke, talking to us about reincarnation, what was about to happen, and what we could expect. He then asked if someone would like to take the chair next to him and be regressed. Now, you would expect every hand to go up, including mine, but as usual, nobody wanted to go first. Everyone laughed, and eventually a lady said, "I'll go first," and she took the empty seat next to him. He asked her to get comfortable and just relax, and in a very gentle way, he talked to her. I can't remember exactly what was said, but I know he was softly spoken, and you could see the lady becoming more and more relaxed. When he felt she was where he wanted her to be, he asked her questions.

"What is your name?"

"Hellen," she replied, in what seemed to be a slightly different voice.

"How old are you?" he asked.

"Twenty-six," she replied.

"What year is it?"

"1865," the lady answers all the questions quickly and with confidence. So, as the regression went on and more answers to the questions were given, I remember sitting there thinking, well, there must be something to this, and I knew I wanted to go next. The lady was eventually taken out of this regression, and when her eyes opened, she had a smile on her face and explained how strange but how nice the experience was.

We were then asked if we had any questions or observations we wanted to discuss. Nearly everyone said how interesting it was and how she seemed so confident with her answers. Until one gentleman in the group put his hand up and explained how certain facts she was stating regarding the period she was claiming to live in were in fact, historically wrong. Well, that took me back to thinking there is no way reincarnation can be proven. I've always said, especially in my field of work, that just because someone says something, you don't have to believe it. The best way is to always get your own experience, and then you have the right to comment. So that's what I did. When asked who wanted to go next, my hand was the first one up, and everyone else found the confidence to join in, wanting their own experience.

I was picked next, and I took my seat. Once again, he talked to me in a very relaxing, meditative way, and I could feel myself becoming more and more absorbed in his words, feeling so relaxed. The only way I can express this sensation is by feeling free. When he felt I was ready, the questions came. "Hello, what's your name?" he asked.

"John," I quickly said.

"How old are you?"

"Eight," I replied.

"What year is it, John?"

"1912" I answered.

"What are you doing, John?"

"I'm working with my dad on our market stall, selling vegetables."

"Where do you live, John?" And with no thought and quick as a flash I said, "Number 3, Iron Street, Horwich."

After a few more questions, he gently brought me back. I remember thinking how strange it was. I knew I was sitting in the church, but I could see and remember everything I was being asked. After a couple more people were regressed, the afternoon eventually ended, and I went home. For a few days, I kept going over what had happened. I was trying to justify everything. Now, I lived in Horwich and worked on the markets, so was that just my conscious thoughts? I had to investigate it more, so I went to the market and asked if they had records of stallholders. They didn't have records, but with a little research, I found that a family by the name I had given had a fruit & veg stall around that time. This amazed me, so I went to the street to see where I would've lived, and that's when I got disappointed. On the street, there were only about ten houses, all on the same side, and the opposite was a garage and an old mill. There was no number 3, just 2,4,6,8,10. Well, that just brought me back to thinking we haven't been here before.

It was a couple of years later, I told someone this story, and they informed me that back in those days, they didn't have odd house numbers on one side of a street and even on another just 1,2,3,4 etc. So, it's possible the house was renumbered. Looking back at this experience, and with all my experiences since, I'm still not convinced. My thoughts seem to think maybe we are taken into such an altered state of consciousness that maybe we are in a state of 'trance,' and it is spirit coming through. Let's just say the jury is still out on that one.

CHAPTER 17

The Young Man

"Life may lead us down different roads, but the bond we share forever holds. Missing you, my cherished brother!"
– Gareth Lewis

I have always enjoyed giving public demonstrations of mediumship, not only in the churches but also in other venues, like civic halls and theatres. Even though what I do is part of the Spiritualist religion, I find sometimes many people don't want to step foot into a church for their own personal reasons. Even though they believe in what we do, they would prefer a more, shall we say, 'commercial venue.' I find at these types of venues; you get a wider variety of people—from true believers in the spirit world to sceptics. You also seem to find younger people attend. It was at one of these venues in Chorley, Lancashire, that I met such people.

Not all demonstrations are easy, and I really don't mind that at all. Otherwise, we would never learn and might even become complacent, letting the ego take over. I always say to my audiences, "Please say 'no' if you don't understand." It makes me work harder and go back to the spirit person for more information. I tell my students that the 'no's' will make you a stronger and even a better Medium.

One evening, as I walked out on to the stage in front about fifty people, I could feel the energy in the room being quite low, with the faces glaring at me, waiting for me to begin. I knew I was going to have to work hard and make the audience feel more at ease. I was just halfway through the demonstration when, out of the corner of my eye, I could see a gentleman, possibly in his late fifties with greying hair, talking and giggling with his friends. I find it very rude when people do this, as it takes me out of the power of working with the spirit world and disturbs the other audience members too. So, I stopped, and looking in the direction of the man, I said, "Everything okay?" With a tone to his voice, he answered, "Yeah!" "Okay, well please don't talk— it's disrupting the evening." And with that, he slumped back in his seat. I just knew that this was not his kind of thing, and he was probably there for a laugh.

The evening was going well, but I must admit that I had struggled in places and felt like I was pulling teeth with some people. Some people have a misconception that you shouldn't say anything at all and let the Medium tell you everything. I don't want the person receiving a message to tell me their life stories— just say if you understand or not. As the evening was ending, I was drawn to a group of young people who had congregated in the back row. I said that I was being drawn to them, and when I could see the shock on their faces as they became slightly red as people turned to see who I was talking to. I told them I sensed the spirit of a young man, and he was drawing me strongly to the young gentleman sitting between the two ladies in the group. As his face glowed with embarrassment, "Me?" he said quietly.

"Yes, I have a young man with me in the spirit world who passed in extremely tragic circumstances and tells me he is your brother." You could hear the gasp as all his friends turned to him, smiling. "That's correct," he said as he sat forward in his seat. I realised he was trying to hold back his emotions from his friends, and trying his best not to give anything away.

I described his brother, telling him how athletic he was and he would look after himself by going to the gym. He just sat and listened, nodding in all the right places. It was when I explained his passing, you could see him taking deep breaths, trying so hard not to cry in front of his friends. I continued by telling him that his brother had passed instantly in an accident on his way home one night and that how he felt so guilty about not being able to say goodbye. He could no longer respond to me as his emotions had taken over, so the young lady next to him confirmed I was correct on his behalf. I felt the presence fade, but I knew there was one last thing he wanted to say: "He will always be with you and love you, and he is so proud of you and how you are back on track." A smile appeared on his face as he said, "Thank you so much, I needed that." And with that, I brought the evening to a close. I left the venue thinking that it had been quite a difficult evening, but overall it had been okay, and the feedback from the audience was positive.

The next day, as I was going through my emails, I saw a message from a lady who was at the event the previous night. Opening it, I realised it was a bit of negative feedback about the demonstration, mainly that I had not given everyone a message. When you have over fifty people in the audience, it's simply not possible to do so. I think she was just upset that I didn't come to her. However, I also got some positive feedback. As I received an email that banished any doubts that I had about the demonstration. It began: "Hello, this is a thank you email. I attended your Psychic Medium evening in Chorley last night. I was invited along to the event at the last minute by a group of friends, and I am so very grateful to them and to you that I went. I was the last person you spoke to, and you gave me a message from my younger brother who died three years ago. You probably thought I reacted strangely and seemed almost uninterested in what you were telling me, but to be honest, it was just that I was astonished and overwhelmed at what I was hearing. But I want you to know that it was the most heart-warming feeling that I have ever had, as you have given me what I have dearly wished for in what has been a very empty three years. You gave me contact with someone who I love and have missed desperately. I feel that you have given me closure and lifted a weight from my life. I feel stronger in myself and would like to thank you from the bottom of my heart for giving me that feeling."

After I read the email, I felt so much better about the demonstration. Although I had also received some criticism, it was this email that made me realise that this is the very reason that I do the job that I do: to be a link between the world of spirit and the physical world, to be a mouthpiece so our loved ones who have passed can say, "I'm still here, and I'm ok."

If I only give one message that means so much to just one person, then I've done my job.

CHAPTER 18

Trolls

"Their darkness can never dim the strength of those who rise above." - Gareth Lewis

I have mentioned before how I was bullied as a child and how it made me feel. You must understand—and I have no doubt that many of you do—that when you are a child and you are the victim of bullies, you feel like you have no control over your life. You can't tell anyone; you've already been warned of the consequences of doing that! So, you keep quiet.

Over the years, my children have both experienced bullying, and so have other members of my family. Whether it's pushing, shoving, name-calling, or actual physical contact, one thing is for sure: it's not nice, and when it's happening to you, it feels as though no one cares. So, you grow up and become an adult. Does it stop? Well, no, but as the years roll by, it takes on a more sinister form, and that form, for me anyway, had been the troll!

This is the faceless bully, the coward who hides behind the anonymity of their online device—be it in the bedroom, the living room, or the shed. One thing you can be sure of is that they are doing it alone, so that there are no witnesses to their vile actions. These people don't have the guts to face up to their victims and are most probably just ordinary people to the world around them. This makes them so dangerous—they could push someone over the edge, and no one would know what they had done.

Maybe they think that it's just a laugh, a bit of fun that's not doing any harm to the target of their malice, but I doubt that very much. I think they know exactly what they are doing, and that's what gives them a kick; they are the bully for the digital age—much more effective and much, much more dangerous!

It was bad enough in the past. When I was a child, I could run home to the safety of my bedroom—a few hours of peace and happiness, no mobile phone, no internet, and no social media. Can you imagine what it must be like for a child victim today? There is no escape—not at school, at home, not anywhere and the sad thing is, it's not just happening to children; it's happening to adults too!

Over the many years that I have been working as a Medium, I have witnessed a vast change in how people behave, and I believe social media has a lot to do with it. Although it can be a very good tool for keeping in touch and for such things as advertising your business, it is also a platform for the keyboard warriors who love to discredit and humiliate their victims. When I see things like this online, it transports me back to the time when I was that frightened little boy, hiding in my bedroom, and feeling that there was not even one person in the world that I could turn to. It makes me think that no matter what I do or where I go, they will never leave me be.

I get home from work, and I could have had the best night ever, but as soon as I turn on the internet, it begins. I know you probably think that I shouldn't look, although it's nice to see the many positive comments that people post, but then amid all the positive comments there will always be that one—the one who wants to criticise and deride everything I do. The worst thing is, it's not just me who's reading it—it's there for the entire world to see. Don't get me wrong; I don't mind a bit of criticism. If it's constructive and not nasty. That's what helps me improve and grow in my work. It's when it's nasty and personal that it hurts. One of the most common ones is, "If he is in contact with the Spirit world, why can't he get next week's lottery numbers?" or "It's all a con to get money out of vulnerable people." I realise it doesn't sound so terrible, but when you are being told that you are a con man and a fraud every time you look online, it really wears you down.

One of the worst comments I have ever had come from a 'born-again Christian.' It was more of a rant than a comment, to be honest. He (or she) began by saying that I was 'blasphemous, and I quote: "You are a disgrace, the epitome of evil, you go against God!" Then he quoted the Bible: "Do not turn to Mediums or Spiritualists, do not seek them out to be defiled by them. I am the Lord your God." (Leviticus 19:31). He continued, "You prey on the vulnerable, and they listen to your un-godly truths. You are one of the Devil's henchmen." To say that I was taken aback by this outburst is an understatement. He did not know me, and for someone who proclaimed himself to be 'religious and God-fearing,' it speaks volumes about the type of person he is! I may not follow his religion, but I believe in God. I also know that I would never use religion as a weapon to discredit or hurt another person, and I am sure that God would be disappointed in anyone who did.

I believe we are all God's children, no matter which faith we choose to follow. When I would talk to Mrs Holden about this matter, she would say 'remember dear' and quote (John 14:1–3): "In my Father's house are many mansions: if it were not so, I would have told you. I go to prepare a place for you. And if I go and prepare a place for you, I will come again, and receive you unto myself; that where I am, there ye may be also." This quote has never left me.

Sometimes, if I have been badly trolled and I can't get the comments out of my mind, I wonder if these people who enjoy calling us 'nut jobs' or charlatans or any other insult they can think of, do they ever sit back and think that although there is good and bad in every religion, and although they may really dislike what I believe in, there is one thing for certain: there has never, ever, been any wars caused by the Spiritualist faith!

CHAPTER 19

The Buxton Stalker

"One who hunts for wickedness should first gaze into their own soul." – Gareth Lewis

In 2019, my mental health had started to slowly take a turn for the worse. Even though my tour was doing great, and demonstrations were selling out, and everything was seeming to be okay on the outside, inside, I wasn't. A few years earlier, I had been diagnosed with Ankylosing Spondylitis (AS), a long-term condition in which the spine and other areas of the body become inflamed. The symptoms of AS can vary but usually involve back pain, stiffness, pain, and swelling in other parts of the body caused by inflammation of the joints (arthritis) and inflammation where a tendon joins a bone. The condition also causes extreme tiredness. Over time, as I was able to do fewer chores around the house and depended more on Kelly, I began once again with that overwhelming feeling of hopelessness and worthlessness.

That year, I had got to where I was struggling to cope and began to self-harm. It got so bad that on one occasion, I stabbed myself several times, resulting in me being taken to hospital and having no choice but to do what I should have done years ago: seek proper medical help. Within a few weeks, I had been to a psychologist and, for the first time, talked about the experiences I had as a child and as an adult. I found those sessions quite hard, especially since I had bottled everything up for all those years.

By the end of the year, my tour was also coming to an end, and I began to plan for the 2020 tour. My first date was going to be at Buxton Conservative Club at the end of January, so I advertised the event as I normally do through social media. This is when something dark and deeply sinister began.

On one post where I was advertising an event, someone commented, saying that what I do is wrong, I'm a charlatan, and that God will strike me down. You know, the usual fanatical criticism of my profession. Feeling fed up and not in a great place, I did something I would not normally do, and in retrospect, wish I hadn't: I shared the post on my page, telling my followers,

"This is what Mediums have to put up with," and this guy needed to 'get a life.' As people commented, agreeing with what I had said, he must have seen what I and others had written, and he was not happy. He seemed upset that I had shared what he had said about me and my work with the world, not caring how much he had upset me. I blocked and ignored him, and thought he would go away. That didn't stop him. He emailed me, not only through my work email address but also through my then-manager's email addresses and my personal email address. All the emails were along the same lines, only now he was threatening to meet me at my show in Buxton.

Enough was enough. I had no choice but to contact the police, but without his details, they couldn't do anything. This was affecting my mental health, and that dark monster (depression) began to take hold again. I felt like I was that child in school, trying to find any way I could to avoid the bullies, but I couldn't. He was effectively in my home, using any media he could to hound me. Then, on New Year's Eve of that year and desperately wanting 2020 to be better, Kelly and I prepared for just a quiet night at home, bringing in 2020. That's when I received a text message from my stalker.

He had somehow got hold of my personal number and harassed me via text. I was just about to block his number when my eldest son, Jack, stopped by to wish us both a Happy New Year before he went out for the evening. He told me not to block him as this now was the only way, after blocking him from every other means, to find out who he was. So, I tried to ignore the messages, when Jack, who had just completed a degree in computer science, came to my aid. Now, don't ask me how or what he did, but he brought up everything he could find out about this man: where he worked, where he lived, and even photographs of him and his family, as the Facebook account he had been using was a fake. "Right," I said, "I'm calling the police!" I was so downtrodden by it all, wondering how someone could make me feel like this—to the point that, on a couple of occasions, I self-harmed and contemplated suicide.

Before I could get my phone to call the police, Jack had taken the stalker's phone number and called the man who was doing this to me. Before I could stop him, Jack took himself into another room. As I stood behind the door, listening, I heard Jack say, "Is that Dave?" He must have said yes, because I could hear Jack's voice getting louder and angrier as he explained who he was. Jack told him what he was doing to his dad. Jack told him he knew everything about him and that if he didn't stop, he would pass it all onto the police. I heard Jack say, "You don't know you are killing my dad by doing what you are doing, as he suffers with his mental health, and I am so worried about him. How would you feel if someone did that to your family? It's so easy to sit behind a computer and bully someone, not knowing or caring how it is affecting them." With that, and with the assurance he would stop, Jack hung up. "You won't be hearing from him again," he said.

I knew I still had to visit Buxton soon to do a demonstration there. I could have cancelled it, but after I thought about everything that had happened, I thought NO! Why should I? If I cancel my demonstration, then he's won, and I have let too many bullies win. Just as a precaution, and in case he turned up, I thought it was right to tell the venue manager what had happened. He asked to see a photograph of him so if he was to turn up, he would not be allowed in, and the police would be called. Knowing that I was safe, and nothing was going to happen, I went on stage that night, confident that the spirit world wouldn't let me down.

CHAPTER 20

The Mother

"It takes true courage to nurture life, boundless strength to raise a child, and endless love to put another's heart before your own." – Gareth Lewis

It was a Saturday afternoon, and in my sitting room, waiting for her mother to arrive, was a young lady called Daniella. I could see she was keen to begin, hopeful we would be able to communicate and that I could bridge the gap between the worlds to deliver a message from one world to another—a message that was so badly needed. Daniella was here because she wanted to communicate with her mother, and now, in my sitting room, was Daniella's mother too. Both were my clients, although in different ways. One sat here with me from this world, and the other here with us in spirit. The mother's name was Michelle, and Daniella was her daughter. The loss of a child is one of the worst pains imaginable, and for this reason, I would like Michelle to tell her story in her words—words which I hope anyone suffering from a loss will find comfort in.

Dearest Gareth,

This recollection comes from a session I had with you very early on. I would say maybe sometime in August 2014.

As you know, my beautiful angel passed on the 3rd of

December 2013. She had just finished school at Manchester High School for Girls and started at Edinburgh University. She was much loved at Manchester High, and when I went to see them in the February after her passing, saying I wanted to have an award in her name given out every year at speech night, the school immediately agreed. In addition, they also wanted to rename the quadrangle outside the school library (central to the school building) "Daniella's Learning Garden" and place a plaque on the wall inscribed with a beautiful poem she had written whilst at school in Year 8. They subsequently set a date for the unveiling ceremony in early September of that year.

I arrived at Gareth's house to have a reading with Gareth just a week or two before the ceremony was to take place. I can't remember everything we discussed, but suddenly, just as we were in mid-conversation, he asked me who Miguel was. Did that name mean anything to me? I said that I didn't know anyone by that name, and I didn't think Daniella did either–the only thing I could think of, and it felt like a very tenuous thought at the time, was that there was a DJ whose music Daniella loved called Miguel. That was the only connection I could make to the name Gareth said to me "Just remember the name Miguel, it may mean something."

When I left the reading that day, I had to go straight to the school to check on all the arrangements for the ceremony, and as I left, driving down Wilbraham Road and stuck at the traffic lights, I got a call from one of Daniella's close friends, called Danielle. She told me she had just had a call from another of Daniella's friends, Neave, and other classmates who oversaw choosing the music for the ceremony. Neave had received an email from the school saying she had to complete the playlist and what were her choices. She immediately phoned Danielle to ask for her opinion on which music Daniella would love the best, and Danielle told me she had replied, 'a particular piece by MIGUEL.'

Danielle was calling me to ask if I was okay with that. In that moment, I knew why Gareth had mentioned Miguel's name to me. It was because Daniella wanted Miguel's music played at the ceremony. I told Danielle about my reading with Gareth and what he had said and thanked her for knowing it was what Daniella wanted. I have a beautiful video of the ceremony with the Miguel track playing, and I always think of Gareth and our session whenever I watch or think of it.

This is just one spectacular and magical example of the many occasions on which we have been together in reading when he has referred to something that no one else in the world could ever have known but Daniella. Even during the last session we did together, he asked me if there were legal documents being discussed about property, and of course, true to form, there had been discussions about having the house I live in transferred into my name. There was no way Gareth could have known about that without Daniella making him aware of it.

More recently, Gareth said that Daniella was drawing his attention to a hollow heart and that I was to look inside it, as there was a message for me in it. There are so many other occasions when Gareth has communicated the most incredible information to me that only Daniella could know.

Thank you beyond words for being there for me, for being my lifeline, and for being the Medium between me and my beautiful, beautiful daughter. I shall always and forever be grateful to you for the greatest gift anyone could ever give me in the circumstances. Thank you beyond words.

This is the hollow heart. The message Daniella wanted to

give is 'Always believe in yourself.' My beautiful angel got me that heart on my birthday just before she passed. How lucky was I, and am I, to have such a wonderful daughter and to have Gareth in my life to remind me that Daniella is still with me, just in a different form.

Michelle's story, a mother's story, is only one of many, and I thank her for her kind words and for allowing me to share her story with you. I think it would only be fitting to let Daniella have the final word: Always believe in yourself.

Daniella's Heart

EPILOGUE

Embracing the Journey

*"My journey has been very exciting, and I love nothing more
than reuniting people with their loved ones and seeing their
face and feeling their emotions that alone is my reward"*
- Gareth Lewis

As I conclude this book, I am reminded of the intricate tapestry
that is life—a weaving together of experiences that shape and
mould us, often leading us down unexpected paths. My journey
has been one of both adversity and profound revelation,
navigating through the realms of spirituality, grappling with the
harrowing effects of bullying, and awakening to the profound
gifts of mediumship. In recounting my spiritual journey, I've
come to understand that the path to enlightenment is not a linear
one but a mosaic of moments—some serene, others turbulent—
each contributing to the evolution of my soul. Through moments
of introspection and encounters with spiritual teachings, I've
unearthed a profound connection with the universe, finding
solace in its mysteries and lessons.

The scars left by bullying were once a source of pain, but
through the healing process, they have become badges of
resilience and strength. In facing adversity, I discovered the
power of compassion, empathy, and the importance of standing
up not only for myself but also for others who might be
experiencing similar trials.

My mediumship is a gift, that has blossomed from the depths of my experiences, has been both enlightening and humbling. Connecting with the spiritual realm has taught me profound truths about life, death, and the disconnect of all souls. It's a responsibility I carry with reverence, offering solace and guidance to those seeking connection with their loved ones beyond the veil.

As I pen these words, I am filled with gratitude for the challenges that pushed me to grow, the kindness that illuminated my path, and the resilience that carried me through moments of darkness. This journey has not been without its trials, yet it has been the crucible in which my spirit found its voice, its purpose.

May this book serve as a testament to the transformative power of perseverance, faith, and the unwavering belief in one's inner light. May it reach those who seek solace, encouragement, or simply a reminder that the tapestry of life, woven with both joy and sorrow, is a masterpiece in its own right.

In closing, I extend my deepest gratitude to every soul who has crossed my path, leaving an indelible mark on my journey. May we all continue to embrace our unique paths, finding beauty in the complexities of our spiritual and human experiences.

Death only ever exists when we forget about our friends and loved ones in spirit.

So always keep them in your hearts, minds, and thoughts, and they will forever walk with you, love you, and guide you.

With upmost gratitude,
Gareth Lewis x